30-MINUTE VEGETARIAN RECIPES

MARY GWYNN'S

30-MINUTE VEGETARIAN RECIPES

Meredith® Press
Des Moines, Iowa

To my husband, Mark

Meredith Press
A division of Meredith Corporation
Des Moines, Iowa

Published in 1995 by Merehurst Limited
Ferry House, 51-57 Lacy Road, Putney, London SW15 1PR

ISBN: 0-696-20615-3
Library of Congress Catalog Card Number: TK

Editor: Beverly Le Blanc
Design: Hammond Hammond
Photographer: Ken Field
Home economist: Louise Pickford
Home economist's assistant: Carol Tennant
Stylist: Suzy Gittins
Typesetter: Michael Weintroub

Colour separation by Global Colour, Malaysia
Printed in Singapore by CS Graphics Pte Ltd

On the cover: Bean and Spring Vegetable Stew, see page 30
On the frontispiece: Mixed Pepper and Mozzarella Bruschetta, see page 18

FOREWORD

Fast food has become an essential in today's busy lives but I really believe that there is no reason why quality and flavor should suffer because of a lack of time. This book represents a slow distillation of the way I have cooked over the past ten years—what has emerged is simple food made from fresh ingredients (and I have to admit, normally prepared in a hurry), enjoyed at leisure by family and friends. So many different people have influenced this personal style; one of the main pleasures I have found from working with food has been that you learn something from everyone you meet or work alongside. Ideas are taken up, adapted and juggled with, to emerge with your own slant. I hope that is exactly what you will do with these recipes. Try them and then develop them to suit your own tastes.

Most of the recipes fit easily into 30 minutes of preparation and cooking time; I certainly don't have more time or inclination in the evening. A couple may just slip over the half hour mark but need little supervision, so you are not standing over them as they cook. All are ideally suited for midweek meals when a single dish served with good bread and a salad is all you need, but they can just as easily be put together to create a most satisfying dinner for friends.

You will find the ingredients are straightforward with a few luxuries thrown in—a selection of basic staples that are always in the cupboard and restocked during my weekly shopping trip, supplemented with whatever is the freshest and most tempting.

For me, cooking without meat has led to a rediscovery of the joys of seasonal vegetables and fruit—the flavors, colors, and tastes highlighted as these ingredients take center stage in each meal.

You will find that most of the recipes serve two to four and a few just one. I know very few people who ever cook for four regularly, and this book reflects that. Also I think it's usually easier to double up on a recipe than it is to divide it in half.

I have never been a fan of already-prepared spice mixes and usually keep a stock of individual spices and mix my own as I need them. However, in recent years the range available has increased so much, as we all cook more exotic dishes on a regular basis, that my cupboard is often overflowing with containers past their use-by date. So with time constraints and a great improvement in the quality of what's available, I do use premixed spices for midweek cooking. Buy the best available—there will be a huge difference in the results.

Mary Gwynn

Introduction

Soups and snacks

Lentils and beans

Pasta dishes

Vegetable dishes and salads

Rice and grain dishes

Egg and cheese dishes

Desserts

INTRODUCTION

A desire for better health has been recognized as one of the major triggers for turning people to a vegetarian diet. However, cutting out meat, be it altogether or just part of the time, will not automatically ensure good health. Recent research that has pinpointed markedly lower rates of cancer and heart disease among vegetarians does not lay all the blame at meat's door. What seems to be behind the figures is that the vegetarian diet is more likely to be high in fresh vegetables and fruit, fiber, and starch and low in saturated fat, all of which puts it into the dietary guidelines set out by the World Health Organization.

Most of the recipes here are based on these recommendations, so use them within the following framework: aim to eat at least five portions of fresh fruit and vegetables a day; eat starches, such as bread, pasta, or rice, with every meal; and remember that fat should make up only 30 percent of your daily intake. (Look for the low-fat symbol, which flags recipes that are 15 grams of fat or less per serving. For desserts, recipes with 5 grams of fat or less are flagged.) Try to avoid the mistake of replacing meat with high-fat dairy products. The Italians have the right idea when they serve huge bowls of pasta topped with small amounts of sauce.

INGREDIENTS GUIDE

I have used readily available ingredients for the recipes in this book as I realize that few people have the time or energy to search out unusual foods unless it's for a special occasion. I do, however, keep a selection of so-called luxury ingredients on hand to add a little interest here and there when I'm cooking in a hurry. Some of them may, at first glance, seem extravagant, but usually they are added to dishes in proportions that are modest compared with their final impact on the finished dish. You can substitute other ingredients, and I have indicated where this will work, but I think that to enjoy vegetarian cooking (in fact, any style of cooking!) to its full scope and range, top-quality basic ingredients are the key.

CHEESES

If you are new to a meat-free diet or are using this book to cook for a vegetarian guest, I want to point out that many cheeses are not suitable for inclusion in a vegetarian diet as they are made with the animal by-product, rennet, which is added during the cheese-making process to coagulate the milk. However, there are increasing numbers of cheeses available made with an alternative.

Most block Parmesan cheese is not suitable but there is an already-grated type from Italy in some supermarkets. As I don't follow a strict vegetarian diet, I always use freshly grated Parmesan cheese, as the wonderful flavor bears no relation to the dry dust of the already-grated canned type. And although fresh Parmesan is expensive, you only need a little. Store the block wrapped in foil or plastic in the cheese drawer of your refrigerator.

OILS

I keep several types of oil in the cupboard; sunflower or canola oil and an extra virgin olive oil for everyday use, and small bottles of walnut and sesame oil for use as flavorings. I have to admit that I use extra virgin oil for everything except Indian or Asian cooking, where the flavor would be too strong. This may seem extravagant but as I save money by not eating meat and basing meals on cheap grains, pasta, and rice, I can justify it to myself. Plus, the flavor and health benefits more than balance the cost. I also keep a bottle of premium bottled extra virgin oil on hand for drizzling over soups, salads, and pasta as a final seasoning. This is expensive—but I use it very sparingly, and only treat myself to an occasional bottle or ask for one as a gift!

BREAD AND BUTTER

There is now a move back to butter as the hydrogenating process used to solidify vegetable and animal fat to make margarine gets the thumbs down from the health experts. I never made the change in the first place—as with many cooks, butter's flavor and versatility for cooking has ensured its place in my kitchen. Still, *moderation is the key,* so I cook with olive oil and use a *little* butter for some sauces and baking, when its flavor is unbeatable. If you prefer, use margarine.

Try to get used to eating bread without butter if you can; this is easy as so many interesting new specialty breads are available. I keep a couple of loaves of my favorites, such as olive, French walnut, and various East Indian-style breads, handy in the freezer to easily be warmed in the oven.

VINEGARS

Balsamic vinegar is aged in wooden casks like a fine wine, which gives it an intense caramel aroma and distinctive sweet-sour taste. It is useful for adding an extra depth of flavor to dressings, casseroles, and sauces. I use a super-market version but the more expensive ones, available from delicatessens and specialty stores, are far superior, so I recommend that you treat yourself to a bottle. Red wine vinegar can be substituted in most recipes.

DRIED VEGETABLES

Dried tomatoes, like balsamic vinegar, have been hailed as the trendy new ingredient of the '90s, and like many fashions, when the fuss dies down they may get relegated to the back of the cupboard. It would, however, be a pity if this were the case with such a versatile ingredient. Add them to soups, pasta sauces, and cheese dishes for a wonderfully intense tomato flavor. They are available either dried or in oil—the dried version needs to be soaked in hot water for 15 minutes before use, and don't waste the soaking liquid because it makes excellent stock. Stored in oil, the reconstituted tomatoes can be sliced and used straight from the jar, ideal for salads and sandwiches. Use the oil in dressings and also for frying.

Dried mushrooms come in different varieties—the range of oddities available in Chinese markets definitely calls for insider knowledge, but ceps (or porcini, as they are known in Italy) are a real plus for meat-free cooking. Reconstituted in the same way as the tomatoes, they have a marvelous rich, earthy flavor that adds a much-needed boost to stocks and heartier dishes. Luckily a little goes a very long way, as dried mushrooms seem on first glance to be prohibitively expensive, but you rarely need more than $\frac{1}{4}$ of an ounce for a dish for four, so do not be put off by the cost.

HERBS

I keep fresh basil growing all year long on my windowsill and grow most of the other herbs I use regularly, such as rosemary, thyme, tarragon, and chives, in pots on the patio. I've never been very successful with parsley, so I buy it weekly and always choose the flat-leaf version, which I consider to have a far superior flavor. If you don't have easy access to fresh herbs, choose the freeze-dried ones—they aren't as good as fresh but are a great improvement over dried. Dill and tarragon are well worth keeping in stock.

Soups and snacks

Quick suppers are what this book is all about, basically one-course meals with something simple to finish. Soups fit perfectly into this category. There are also times when I want to serve a simple starter, or just want something on a tray. The recipes in this chapter are for these occasions.

SUMMER VEGETABLE SOUP WITH PESTO

Time to make: about 5 minutes
Time to cook: 25 minutes

Serves 2

½ **small onion (¼ cup)**

½ **stalk celery (¼ cup)**

½ **garlic clove**

1 **tomato**

½ **small carrot**

1 **small potato**

2 **ounces Savoy cabbage,
   about ½ cup**

2 **ounces green beans,
   about ½ cup**

2 **ounces broccoli, about ½ cup**

1 **tablespoon olive oil**

2½ **cups vegetable stock
   or broth**

**Salt and freshly ground
   black pepper**

¼ **cup macaroni**

1½ **tablespoons pesto sauce**

**Freshly grated Parmesan
   cheese**

R eally expensive, first-pressed extra virgin olive oil should be used sparingly, like a seasoning, rather than for frying or in mayonnaise. I find that a dash of my favorite extra virgin olive oil added just before serving really enhances the flavor of the pesto in this fresh-tasting soup. Warm olive bread is delicious with this.

1   To prepare the vegetables, chop the onion, celery, garlic, and tomato. Peel and dice the carrot and potato. Shred the cabbage, then cut the green beans and broccoli into short lengths.
2   Heat the oil in a large saucepan over medium heat. Add the onion, celery, carrot, and garlic and cook, stirring occasionally, for 3 minutes until softened but not browned.
3   Stir in the cabbage, green beans, and broccoli, and continue cooking 2 minutes more.
4   Stir in the tomato, stock, salt, and pepper. Bring to a boil, then lower the heat and simmer 10 minutes until the vegetables are almost tender.
5   Stir in the pasta, increase the heat slightly and continue simmering 10 minutes more until the pasta is tender.
6   Stir in the pesto; check the seasonings and sprinkle with grated Parmesan.

Cook's Tip
You can use any type of vegetables for this soup. I tend to buy a variety to use in dishes such as this, but what actually goes in each soup varies every time I make it.

Nutrition facts per serving: 322 calories, 18 g total fat (1 g saturated fat), 7 mg cholesterol, 1,435 mg sodium, 40 g carbohydrate, 5 g fiber, 10 g protein.
Daily Values: 47% vitamin A, 78% vitamin C, 10% calcium, 15% iron.

Stirring in the pesto sauce

CHILI BEAN SOUP

Time to make: about 10 minutes
Time to cook: 20 minutes

Serves 2

1 small red onion

1 small garlic clove

1 15-ounce can red
   kidney beans

1 tablespoon olive oil

½ teaspoon chili powder

½ teaspoon ground cumin

1 to 2 tablespoons
   tomato paste

2 teaspoons lemon juice

1 tablespoon Worcestershire
   sauce (optional)

Few drops hot pepper sauce

2½ cups vegetable stock
   or broth

Salt and freshly ground black
   pepper

Topping

1 ounce vegetarian
   cheddar cheese

4 slices French bread

This recipe first appeared in the pages of a vegetarian magazine and it was so popular that I've included it here. It freezes well but the chili flavor intensifies the longer you keep it, so use less chili powder if you intend to make extra for your freezer.

1   To prepare the vegetables, chop the onion and mince the garlic. Drain and rinse the kidney beans.
2   Heat the oil in a large saucepan over medium heat. Add the onion and garlic and cook 3 minutes until softened but not browned.
3   Stir in the kidney beans, chili powder, cumin, tomato paste, lemon juice, Worcestershire sauce, hot pepper sauce, and stock. Bring to a boil, then lower the heat, cover and simmer for 15 minutes. Cool slightly.
4   Transfer soup to a blender or food processor and puree the soup, *half* at a time, until smooth, then return it to the cleaned pan. Reheat it but do not allow it to boil. Season to taste.
5   Meanwhile, shred the cheese for the topping. Preheat broiler.
6   Sprinkle the slices of bread with the cheese. Broil for 1 to 2 minutes or until cheese melts. Ladle the hot soup into individual bowls. Place toasted bread atop soup and serve.

Cook's Tip
If you think you will be rushed at mealtime, you can puree the soup up to 2 days ahead and store it covered in the refrigerator. To serve, just reheat the soup and continue as directed.

Nutrition facts per serving: 415 calories, 11 g total fat (1 g saturated fat), 0 mg cholesterol, 2,105 mg sodium, 72 g carbohydrate, 13 g fiber, 25 g protein.
Daily Values: 9% vitamin A, 13% vitamin C, 19% calcium, 37% iron.

GREEN RICE SOUP

Time to make: about 5 minutes
Time to cook: 20 to 25 minutes

Serves 2

½ **small onion**

1 **small turnip**

1 **small carrot**

6 **ounces Chinese cabbage**

2½ **cups vegetable stock
    or broth**

1 **tablespoon olive oil**

4 **or 5 strands saffron**

**Salt and freshly ground
    black pepper**

¼ **cup arborio rice**

**Extra virgin olive oil and
    freshly grated Parmesan
    cheese, if desired**

Both the Italians and Spanish have versions of this soup. Short-grain rice is grown in abundance in both countries, giving the national rice dishes their individual characteristics—Italian risottos (made with arborio rice) and Spanish paellas both have creamy textures with a wonderful firm bite to the rice. I use arborio rice in this soup as more authentic Spanish rice is not so readily available, but you can also use a long-grain white rice and the cooking time will be reduced to 12 to 15 minutes.

1   To prepare the vegetables, finely chop the onion and peel and dice the turnip and carrot. Remove any tough cores from the spring cabbage and discard; shred the cabbage.
2   In a small saucepan, over medium heat, heat the stock until it is simmering.
3   Meanwhile, heat the oil in a large saucepan over medium heat. Add the onion and cook 3 minutes, stirring occasionally, until softened but not browned. Stir in the turnip, carrot, and cabbage and continue simmering until the greens wilt.
4   Mix the saffron with 1½ tablespoons of the simmering stock in a small heatproof bowl, then add it to the pan along with the remaining stock, salt, and pepper.
5   Bring the mixture to a boil, then stir in the rice, lower the heat and simmer 15 to 20 minutes until the rice is tender. Check the seasonings and, if desired, serve with extra virgin olive oil and freshly grated Parmesan.

Cook's Tip
Swiss chard is an excellent substitute for the Chinese cabbage in this soup if you can find it or grow your own.

Nutrition facts per serving: 188 calories, 8 g total fat (1 g saturated fat), 0 mg cholesterol, 1,278 mg sodium, 33 g carbohydrate, 4 g fiber, 3 g protein.
Daily Values: 67% vitamin A, 66% vitamin C, 4% calcium, 10% iron.

BROILED TOMATO SOUP
WITH TARRAGON

Time to make: 10 minutes
Time to cook: 10 minutes

Serves 2

**2 large beef tomatoes, about
    1 pound**

6 green onions

1 large slice white bread

1 or 2 garlic cloves

1 teaspoon tomato paste

**2 tablespoons chopped fresh
    tarragon**

1 teaspoon red wine vinegar

1¼ cups tomato juice

⅔ cup iced water

**1 tablespoon extra virgin
    olive oil**

**Salt and freshly ground
    black pepper**

**Tarragon leaves and diced
    cucumber, to garnish**

When the weather starts to get warm, my husband starts asking for gazpacho, the wonderfully refreshing Spanish chilled tomato soup.

This is an emergency version created when the only salad vegetables I had in the refrigerator were tomatoes. Broiling or roasting tomatoes really brings out the full flavor that may otherwise be lacking in many of the store-bought specimens. I usually make this cold soup with beef tomatoes but substitute Italian plum tomatoes when I can get them.

1 Preheat the broiler to high. To prepare the vegetables, halve the tomatoes and chop the green onions.
2 Arrange the tomatoes, skin sides down, on the broiler pan and broil about 10 minutes, turning them over after 5 minutes, until the skins are blackened all over and all the flesh is soft.
3 Meanwhile, cut the crusts off the bread and mince the garlic cloves.
4 Scoop the tomato flesh into a blender or food processor. Add the bread, garlic, tomato paste, tarragon, vinegar, tomato juice, water, and olive oil; process until smooth. Check the seasonings and chill until ready to serve.
5 To serve, garnish with tarragon leaves and diced cucumber and serve with crusty bread.

Cook's Tip
To chill this soup quickly, serve it with a couple of ice cubes floating on top.

Nutrition facts per serving: 177 calories, 8 g total fat (1 g saturated fat), 0 mg cholesterol, 711 mg sodium, 26 g carbohydrate, 5 g fiber, 5 g protein.
Daily Values: 31% vitamin A, 132% vitamin C, 5% calcium, 20% iron.

*Broiled Tomato Soup with Tarragon
served with Broiled Eggplant on
French Bread with Tomato Salsa (see
page 20)*

WINTER VEGETABLE BROTH

Time to make: 5 minutes
Time to cook: 25 to 50 minutes

Serves 2

1 small onion
1 small carrot
1 small turnip
½ small rutabaga
½ leek
½ tablespoon olive oil
1 ounce pearl barley
2½ cups vegetable stock
Salt and freshly ground black pepper
Chopped fresh parsley, to garnish

Pearl barley gives flavor and texture to this simple soup, but adding it does push the cooking time over the 30-minute mark. However, I've included the barley because it adds valuable protein to the dish, but leave it out if you don't have the time. Instead, just cook the vegetables for 20 minutes and serve this soup with whole-wheat bread and cheese for a balanced meal.

1 To prepare the vegetables, chop the onion, finely cube the carrot, turnip and rutabaga, and slice the leek.
2 Heat the oil in a large pan, then add the onion, carrot, turnip, rutabaga, and leek and cook over medium heat 3 to 4 minutes without browning. Add the barley and continue cooking 1 minute.
3 Stir in the stock and seasonings and bring to a boil, then lower the heat, cover and simmer 45 minutes until the barley and vegetables are tender. Adjust the seasonings and serve in bowls sprinkled with parsley.

Cook's Tip
This recipe also makes a tasty smooth soup. Just omit the barley and puree the cooked vegetables and stock in a blender or food processor until smooth. Stir in 6 tablespoons light cream and serve sprinkled with chopped chives.

Nutrition facts per serving: 123 calories, 5 g total fat (1 g saturated fat), 0 mg cholesterol, 1,266 mg sodium, 25 g carbohydrate, 6 g fiber, 3 g protein.
Daily Values: 66% vitamin A, 19% vitamin C, 3% calcium, 10% iron.

THICK LEEK AND LENTIL SOUP

Time to make: 10 minutes
Time to cook: 25 minutes

Serves 2

½ large onion

1½ stalks celery

1 carrot

1 large leek

1½ tablespoons olive oil

½ tablespoon tomato paste

Generous ⅓ cup red lentils

2½ cups vegetable stock

2 cloves

1 small bay leaf

½ teaspoon Worcestershire
    sauce or soy sauce

Salt and freshly ground
    black pepper

Finely chopped fresh parsley,
    to garnish

Soup, bread, and cheese make up a standard winter Saturday lunch in my house, and I often make double quantities of this soup and freeze it to use the extra for the kids' school lunches. The red lentils make this a tasty, filling soup.

1 To prepare the vegetables, slice the onion, celery, carrot, and leek.
2 Heat the oil in a large saucepan, add the onion, celery, carrot, and leek and cook over medium heat, stirring occasionally, until softened but not browned.
3 Stir in the tomato paste, lentils, stock, cloves, bay leaf, Worcestershire or soy sauce, and seasonings. Bring to a boil, then lower the heat and simmer, half covered, until the lentils are tender, about 20 minutes.
4 Transfer the soup to a blender or food processor and puree until smooth, then return to the rinsed-out pan. Reheat the soup, but do not boil. Check the soup for seasonings, then serve in a large bowl and sprinkle with parsley.

Cook's Tip

Use any bean in this soup instead of the lentils, as long as you use a canned variety so it doesn't need lengthy soaking and cooking. I have been very happy with the results when I have used canned pinto beans and navy beans.

Nutrition facts per serving: 268 calories, 12 g total fat (1 g saturated fat), 0 mg cholesterol, 1,316 mg sodium, 40 g carbohydrate, 7 g fiber, 11 g protein.
Daily Values: 76% vitamin A, 24% vitamin C, 7% calcium, 36% iron.

MIXED PEPPER AND MOZZARELLA BRUSCHETTA

Time to make: 5 to 10 minutes
Time to grill: about 10 minutes

Serves 2

½ red bell pepper

½ yellow bell pepper

1 small red onion

5 ounces mozzarella or
    goat cheese

3 tablespoons olive oil

1 tablespoon chopped fresh
    oregano

2 large slices bread, such
    as French

1 garlic clove, halved

Salt and freshly ground
    black pepper

This is my version of open sandwiches with a distinctly Italian taste. I use whatever firm bread I have on hand, although a coarse-textured bread soaks up the juices best. This recipe makes a luxurious but simple snack lunch, and my pepper-loving children adore it.

1 Preheat broiler to high. To prepare the vegetables, core and seed the red and yellow pepper halves. Cut the onion in half.
2 Under the hot broiler, broil the peppers and onion on both sides until blackened all over. Place the peppers in a plastic bag 2 minutes for the skins to soften, then skin and cut into strips. Slice the onion. Coarsely grate or crumble the cheese.
3 Put the pepper and onion slices in a bowl with half the olive oil, the oregano, cheese, and seasonings.
4 Toast the bread on both sides under the broiler, then rub one side of each slice with the cut garlic clove.
5 Drizzle with the remaining oil and top with the pepper mixture. Serve immediately.

Cook's Tips
I always use my best extra virgin olive oil for bruschetta as the flavor makes all the difference. In fact, you can serve the toasted bread simply rubbed with garlic and then drizzled with the oil for a delicious snack. For a new twist, I sometimes add one shredded dried tomato in oil to the mix, or 3 or 4 coarsely chopped black olives or capers, or a mixture of both.

Nutrition facts per serving: 524 calories, 37 g total fat (12 g saturated fat), 55 mg cholesterol, 596 mg sodium, 30 g carbohydrate, 1 g fiber, 18 g protein.
Daily Values: 31% vitamin A, 106% vitamin C, 34% calcium, 12% iron.

Mixed Pepper and Mozzarella
Bruschetta

BROILED EGGPLANT ON BREAD WITH TOMATO SALSA

Time to make: 5 to 10 minutes
Time to broil: 10 to 15 minutes

Serves 2

1 eggplant, about 8 ounces
½ garlic clove
2 tablespoons olive oil
1 tablespoon chopped fresh mint
Salt and freshly ground black pepper
½ loaf olive bread or French bread

Tomato Salsa

½ green chili
1 plum tomato
1 green onion

Photograph, page 15

This dish works well on the barbecue as the eggplant picks up a wonderful smoky flavor from the coals. But if you're not having a barbecue, don't worry because it is still good prepared under the broiler, as the mint-flavored oil gives its own kick.

1 Preheat the broiler to high. To prepare the eggplant, cut it lengthwise into slices about ¼ inch thick. Chop the garlic.
2 Put the oil, garlic, mint, salt, and pepper in a bowl and mix together.
3 Arrange the eggplant slices on the broiler pan and brush with half the oil mixture. Broil about 5 minutes until golden, then turn the slices over and brush the other side. Broil again until golden.
4 Meanwhile, make the tomato salsa. Seed the chili. Put the chili, the tomato, green onion, salt, and pepper in a blender or food processor, and process until chopped; the salsa should be quite coarse, not a puree.
5 Split the bread in half horizontally, then each piece in half again. Toast on both sides under the broiler.
6 Arrange the eggplant slices on top of the slices of toast. Serve with the tomato salsa.

Cook's Tip
I also use this method to make a quick eggplant and pepper salad. Make up extra oil mixture and brush it over halved peppers, then broil them alongside the eggplant. Layer the vegetables in a serving dish and let stand until the vegetables are at room temperature before serving.

Nutrition facts per serving: 488 calories, 18 g total fat (3 g saturated fat), 0 mg cholesterol, 799 mg sodium, 70 g carbohydrate, 3 g fiber, 12 g protein.
Daily Values: 4% vitamin A, 34% vitamin C, 9% calcium, 31% iron.

SPICED CASHEWS AND ALMONDS

Time to make: 2 minutes
Time to cook: 5 minutes

Serves 4

1 large clove garlic

2 tablespoons sunflower oil

Dash ground red pepper

¼ teaspoon ground cumin

¼ teaspoon ground coriander

½ cup unsalted cashews

½ cup blanched almonds

Coarse sea salt

I am never organized enough to make dainty little predinner nibbles when we entertain, and I stopped buying various large bags of chips when I realized it was all too easy to get through a bag all on my own before anyone else arrived! So, friends usually get a bowl of dry-roasted nuts or a slice or two of toasted baguette spread with black olive paste. If they are very fortunate, however, I make these spicy nuts. I think these are ideal because I have the ingredients on hand and they are incredibly quick to prepare. They also go well as a side dish with a vegetable curry or the biryani on page 70.

1   Thinly slice the garlic, then cut it into slivers.
2   Heat the oil in a skillet until almost smoking, then add the garlic, red pepper, cumin, and coriander, and stir until the garlic is golden, or about 30 seconds.
3   Add the nuts and stir over medium heat until they are golden brown, about 3 to 4 minutes. Take care not to let them burn.
4   Remove the nuts from the pan with a slotted spoon and drain well on paper towels. Sprinkle with sea salt and serve warm or at room temperature.

Cook's Tip
Use any selection of nuts for this recipe as long as they haven't been presalted or roasted. I have also made this recipe using whole cumin seeds, which add an interesting texture.

Nutrition facts per serving: 196 calories, 17 g total fat (3 g saturated fat), 0 mg cholesterol, 37 mg sodium, 9 g carbohydrate, 3 g fiber, 6 g protein.
Daily Values: 0% vitamin A, 0% vitamin C, 4% calcium, 13% iron.

Lentils and beans

The current interest in peasant-style cuisines has propelled humble lentils and beans into some of the smartest kitchens. My kitchen may not be one of the latter but we do eat lots of lentils and beans.

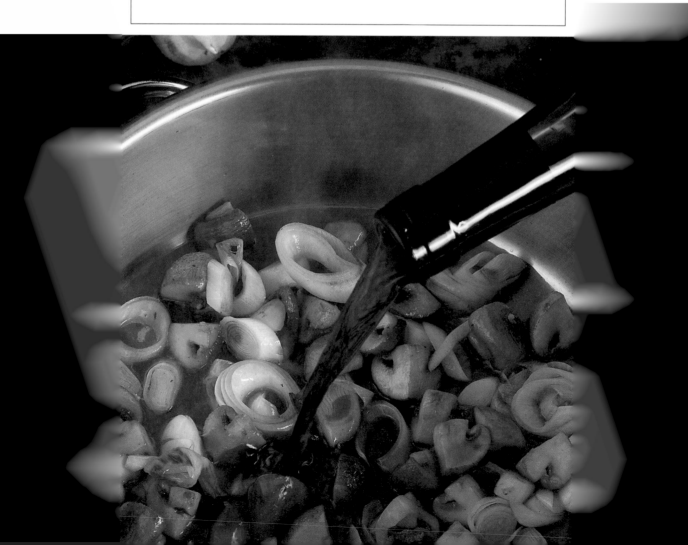

LENTILS AND MUSHROOMS IN RED WINE

LOW-FAT

Time to make: about 5 minutes
Time to cook: about 25 minutes

Serves 2

---

1 leek

½ garlic clove

1 cup fresh mushrooms

1 tablespoon olive oil

5 tablespoons red wine

1½ tablespoons chopped fresh parsley

½ tablespoon chopped fresh thyme

½ teaspoon Dijon-style mustard

3 tablespoons tomato puree

1 tablespoon Worcestershire sauce or soy sauce

2 cups cooked lentils (see Note, page 24)

Salt and freshly ground black pepper

Chopped fresh parsley, to garnish

In this dish, mushrooms make a rich-tasting stew with lentils and red wine, just the food for a cold, wintry evening if served with creamy mashed potatoes. Brown mushrooms (or chestnut or crimini mushrooms) have an intensity of flavor often lacking in the common white variety. I always buy them for any dish that requires unspecified mushrooms.

1 To prepare the vegetables, slice the leek, then rinse it in plenty of cold water and drain well. Mince the garlic and slice the mushrooms.
2 Heat the oil in a saucepan over medium heat. Add the leek and garlic and cook 3 minutes, stirring occasionally, until the leek is softened but not browned.
3 Stir in the sliced mushrooms, turn up the heat and continue cooking, stirring occasionally, until they are lightly browned, 5 minutes.
4 Stir in the wine, chopped parsley and thyme, mustard, tomato puree, and Worcestershire or soy sauce, and season well. Bring to a boil, then simmer 10 minutes, stirring occasionally.
5 Stir the lentils into the mushroom mixture and continue simmering 5 minutes more to heat through. If there is a lot of liquid, turn up the heat and boil the mixture rapidly to reduce the liquid. Check the seasonings and garnish with parsley.

Nutrition facts per serving: 363 calories, 8 g total fat (1 g saturated fat), 0 mg cholesterol, 274 mg sodium, 51 g carbohydrate, 13 g fiber, 20 g protein.
Daily Values: 5% vitamin A, 32% vitamin C, 6% calcium, 59% iron.

Adding the red wine to the leek, garlic, and mushrooms

LENTIL AND BROILED RED PEPPER SALAD

LOW-FAT

Time to make: 10 to 15 minutes
Time to broil: about 5 minutes

Serves 2

½ **red sweet pepper or ½ of a 7-ounce jar roasted red sweet peppers, chopped**

½ **red onion**

1 **garlic clove**

2 **cups cooked lentils***

1 **tablespoon chopped fresh flat-leaf parsley**

½ **lemon**

1 **tablespoon red wine vinegar**

2 **tablespoons olive oil**

Salt and freshly ground black pepper

Lentils and beans, with their soaking and cooking times, may not seem like ideal ingredients for an instant supper but they play such an important role in a balanced, meat-free diet that it would be a pity not to use them. If you want to substitute canned beans in these recipes, however, use a 14- to 15-ounce can, rinsed and drained.

1 Preheat broiler to high. To prepare the vegetables, core and seed the pepper half. Finely chop the onion and mince the garlic.
2 Arrange the pepper half, cut side down, on the broiler pan and broil until the skin is blackened all over, then turn it over and continue broiling until blackened on the inside. Place the pepper in a plastic bag for 2 minutes, then skin it and dice the flesh. Place the roasted pepper in a bowl.
3 Meanwhile, drain and rinse the lentils and add them to the pepper, along with the chopped onion, garlic, and parsley.
4 Finely grate the lemon rind into another small bowl, then add the vinegar, olive oil, salt, and pepper, and whisk together until well mixed.
5 Pour the dressing over the lentils and stir gently until well combined, then cover and chill until ready to serve.

*Note
To cook the lentils, rinse about ⅔ cup lentils; place them in a saucepan with 1⅓ cups water. Bring to boiling; reduce heat. Simmer, covered, for 15 to 20 minutes (for green and yellow varieties) or 3 to 5 minutes (for red varieties). Drain.

Nutrition facts per serving: 370 calories, 14 g total fat (2 g saturated fat), 0 mg cholesterol, 74 mg sodium, 45 g carbohydrate, 10 g fiber, 19 g protein.
Daily Values: 15% vitamin A, 69% vitamin C, 4% calcium, 47% iron.

SPICED RED LENTILS WITH CABBAGE

LOW-FAT

Time to make: about 5 minutes
Time to cook: 25 to 30 minutes

Serves 2

1 small onion

1 garlic clove

½ pound white cabbage

2 tablespoons olive oil

1 teaspoon coriander seeds

½ teaspoon caraway seeds

½ cup red lentils

½ cup tomato puree

1¼ cups vegetable stock
  or broth

Salt and freshly ground
  black pepper

Chopped flat-leaf parsley,
  to garnish

Lentils and cabbage make a hearty and satisfying partnership which I utilize in all kinds of ways. This version is lightly spiced and makes a very simple supper on a cold night. Add extra stock and you can turn it into a soup. To finish the meal, I usually serve this with baked potatoes or rice.

1 To prepare the vegetables, finely slice the onion, mince the garlic, and shred the cabbage.
2 Heat the oil in a saucepan over medium heat. Add the onion and garlic and cook 3 minutes, stirring occasionally, until the onion is softened but not browned.
3 Stir in the the coriander seeds, caraway seeds, and cabbage and continue cooking 5 minutes until the cabbage wilts. Meanwhile, pick over the lentils, if necessary.
4 Stir in the tomato puree, lentils, stock, salt, and pepper. Bring to a boil, then cover and simmer 15 to 20 minutes, stirring occasionally, until the lentils are tender and soft and the mixture is thick. Add more stock or water if the lentils get too dry.
5 Check the seasonings and garnish with chopped flat-leaf parsley.

Cook's Tip
Red and green lentils are the only legumes that don't need to be presoaked before you can use them, so they are very useful for the cook in a hurry. Green lentils work just as well as the red lentils in this dish but will take a little longer to cook.

Nutrition facts per serving: 297 calories, 15 g total fat (2 g saturated fat), 0 mg cholesterol, 920 mg sodium, 37 g carbohydrate, 5 g fiber, 11 g protein.
Daily Values: 11% vitamin A, 131% vitamin C, 8% calcium, 32% iron.

CREAMY PUY LENTILS WITH LEMON DRESSING

LOW-FAT

Time to make: about 5 minutes
Time to cook: about 30 minutes

Serves 2

½ cup Puy lentils

1 garlic clove

1 small tomato

4 pitted black olives

1 tablespoon cooking oil
   or butter

½ lemon

2 teaspoons chopped
   fresh tarragon

½ teaspoon stone ground
   mustard

1 to 2 tablespoons crème
   fraîche (see Note, page 87)
   or yogurt

Salt and freshly ground
   black pepper

Chopped flat-leaf parsley,
   tarragon sprigs, and lemon
   wedges, to garnish

This salad can be served hot or at room temperature—either way, it has a subtle, earthy flavor that is a change from some of the stronger Mediterranean dishes that are so popular these days. I always use Puy lentils for simple recipes like this, where the lentils are not overpowered by spices, as they have a lovely distinctive flavor and keep their shape and texture when cooked.

These lentils take about half an hour to cook, so when I am preparing this after work, I put the lentils on to simmer, then put the children to bed and read them stories. By then the lentils are ready for me to finish the dish.

1 Put the lentils in a saucepan over high heat. Cover with cold water and bring to a boil. Boil rapidly 10 minutes. Lower the heat and simmer gently until the lentils are just tender, about 20 minutes. Drain well.
2 Meanwhile, prepare the vegetables and make the dressing. Chop the garlic. Seed and chop the tomato and halve the olives.
3 While the lentils are still cooking, heat the oil or butter in a small skillet over medium heat. Add the garlic and fry about 1½ minutes, stirring occasionally, until it just begins to turn brown. Grate in the lemon rind, then stir in the juice. Add the tarragon and mustard and continue cooking 30 seconds, stirring, then stir in the crème fraîche or yogurt, salt, and pepper. Bring to a boil, then stir in the drained lentils, tomato, and olives.
4 Transfer the lentils to a serving dish, garnish and serve immediately, or set aside to cool to room temperature.

Cook's Tip
Brown lentils are fine if you can't find Puy lentils, but take care not to overcook them, as they will become mushy.

Nutrition facts per serving: 218 calories, 11 g total fat (6 g saturated fat), 25 mg cholesterol, 193 mg sodium, 24 g carbohydrate, 2 g fiber, 10 g protein.
Daily Values: 12% vitamin A, 31% vitamin C, 3% calcium, 23% iron.

Creamy Puy Lentils with Lemon Dressing

GREEN LENTILS WITH GARLIC AND CILANTRO

LOW-FAT

Time to make: about 5 minutes
Time to cook: 12 to 15 minutes

Serves 2

½ small onion

1 garlic clove

1-inch piece fresh gingerroot

Small bunch fresh cilantro

½ tablespoon sunflower oil

1 teaspoon cumin seeds

⅔ cup dried green lentils

½ tablespoon lemon juice

Dash ground red pepper

Salt

I cook Indian food at least once a week, normally on the nights when I come home from work not knowing what's in the refrigerator but confident that there will be a package of lentils, some basmati rice, and a selection of spices in the cupboard. Mahdur Jaffrey has been my guiding light since I started cooking this way—her recipes always work perfectly and she offers lots of good advice on how to put dishes together to make a meal. Her *Indian Cookery* is one of the most used books in my kitchen and it has given me the confidence to start experimenting for myself with spices and ingredients. Serve this lentil dish with rice, bread, and a fresh onion and tomato relish. For a more elaborate meal, you can also prepare the Egg and Cauliflower Curry on page 82.

1 To prepare the vegetables, chop the onion and mince the garlic. Peel and finely chop the ginger and finely chop the cilantro.

2 Heat the oil in a saucepan over medium heat. Add the onion and garlic and cook about 5 minutes, stirring occasionally, until the onion is softened and lightly browned. Stir in the cumin seeds and chopped ginger and cook 1 minute more.

3 Stir in the chopped cilantro; cook and stir until it wilts. Stir in 1¼ cups cold water and the lentils. Reduce the heat. Cover and simmer 35 to 40 minutes until the lentils are tender, adding water during cooking, if necessary. Add the lemon juice, red pepper, and salt; simmer 5 minutes more, stirring occasionally.

4 Check the seasonings and serve.

Nutrition facts per serving: 158 calories, 4 g total fat (0 g saturated fat), 0 mg cholesterol, 72 mg sodium, 22 g carbohydrate, 5 g fiber, 9 g protein.
Daily Values: 0% vitamin A, 7% vitamin C, 2% calcium, 27% iron.

SPICY BEAN HOT POT

Time to make: 5 minutes
Time to cook: about 25 minutes

Serves 2

---

1 onion

½ garlic clove

1 tablespoon olive oil

1 teaspoon ground cumin

1 7½-ounce can tomatoes (undrained), chopped

1 tablespoon tomato paste

Few drops hot pepper sauce

Salt and freshly ground black pepper

½ of a 15-ounce can red kidney beans, drained

½ of a 15-ounce can pinto beans, drained

½ of a 15-ounce can white kidney beans (cannellini), drained

Chopped fresh parsley, to garnish

M y husband, who is no mean cook, tested this recipe for me and has cooked it several times since for skeptical, meat-eating friends. A hot pot, as the English call it, is generally a meat and vegetable stew. Obviously, this is a vegetarian version. Served with garlic bread and a green salad, it has transformed even the most rampant carnivore, if not into an instant convert, at least into someone willing to acknowledge that vegetarian food tastes better than they expected. For the family, I serve this with baked potatoes and a salad.

1 Slice the onion and mince the garlic.
2 Heat the olive oil in a medium saucepan. Add the onion, garlic, and cumin. Cook over medium heat 3 minutes or until softened.
3 Stir in the undrained tomatoes, tomato paste, hot pepper sauce, and seasonings to taste. Cover and simmer gently 10 minutes, stirring occasionally.
4 Add the beans to the sauce, then simmer, covered, 10 minutes more, until the sauce has thickened. Adjust the seasonings and sprinkle with parsley. Serve immediately.

Cook's Tip
For a tasty addition, brush thin slices of French bread with olive oil, toast them until golden, then top each serving with a slice.

Nutrition facts per serving: 323 calories, 8 g total fat (1 g saturated fat), 0 mg cholesterol, 965 mg sodium, 55 g carbohydrate, 17 g fiber, 20 g protein. **Daily Values:** 8% vitamin A, 37% vitamin C, 11% calcium, 41% iron.

BEAN AND SPRING VEGETABLE STEW

Time to make: about 5 minutes
Time to cook: about 25 minutes

Serves 2

| 1 small leek |
| 1 small garlic clove |
| 2 ounces baby carrots |
| 2 ounces turnips or baby turnips |
| ½ small cauliflower |
| Salt and freshly ground black pepper |
| ½ cup green beans |
| 1 tablespoon olive oil |
| 1 7½-ounce can tomatoes (undrained), chopped |
| ¼ cup dry white wine |
| ½ tablespoon chopped fresh rosemary |
| Salt and freshly ground black pepper |
| 1 cup canned small white or Great Northern beans |
| Fresh rosemary sprigs, to garnish |

This stew would once have been served only in the spring as the new vegetables came in, but now baby vegetables can be found just about all year around. Yet, I still enjoy the joys of seasonal produce. That's when I cook this to get the very best flavor.

1 To prepare the vegetables, slice the leek, then rinse it in cold water and drain well. Chop the garlic. Trim the carrots and turnips and lightly scrape the skins if necessary. (If using regular size turnips, cut into quarters.) Break the cauliflower into flowerets and halve the green beans crosswise.

2 Heat the oil in a large saucepan over medium heat. Add the leek and garlic and cook 3 minutes, stirring occasionally, until the leek is softened but not brown.

3 Add the carrots, turnips, undrained tomatoes, wine, rosemary, salt, and pepper. Bring to a boil, then lower the heat and simmer 10 minutes.

4 Add the drained and rinsed beans, cauliflower flowerets, and green beans. Cover and simmer 10 minutes until all the vegetables are just tender. Check the seasonings and serve immediately, garnished with rosemary.

Cook's Tip

This stew is quite full of vegetables with just a little liquid. If you like a juicier stew, add a 6-ounce can of tomato juice along with the wine before simmering.

Nutrition facts per serving: 223 calories, 8 g total fat (1 g saturated fat), 0 mg cholesterol, 474 mg sodium, 33 g carbohydrate, 11 g fiber, 10 g protein.
Daily Values: 73% vitamin A, 94% vitamin C, 10% calcium, 23% iron.

Bean and Spring Vegetable Stew (see photo, front cover) served with Spiced Garbanzo Beans with Spinach (see page 32)

SPICED GARBANZO BEANS WITH SPINACH

LOW-FAT

Time to make: about 5 minutes
Time to cook: 25 minutes

Serves 4

**12 ounces fresh leaf spinach, or
½ of a 9-ounce package
frozen leaf spinach, thawed**

1 small onion

1 garlic clove

2 tablespoons sunflower oil

**1 teaspoon grated fresh
gingerroot**

2 teaspoons ground coriander

1 teaspoon ground cumin

Dash ground turmeric

1 dried chili, chopped

**1 7½-ounce can tomatoes
(undrained), chopped**

1 15-ounce can garbanzo beans

½ teaspoon salt

**1 teaspoon garam masala
(an Indian spice mix),
see Cook's Tip at right**

See page 31, top of photograph

Canned garbanzo beans are an essential standby in my kitchen and often make the basis of a quick supper dish. Here they are paired up with spinach, for a nutritionally sound combination of textures and tastes. I serve this with basmati rice cooked with a little turmeric in the water, which gives it a rich yellow color.

1   To prepare the vegetables, if you are using fresh spinach that is not prewashed, rinse well in several changes of cold water, then shake dry. Remove the thick central veins, then finely shred the leaves. Chop the onion and mince the garlic.

2   Heat the oil in a large saucepan over medium heat. Add the onion, garlic, and ginger and cook 5 minutes, stirring occasionally, until the onion is softened and golden.

3   Stir in the coriander, cumin, turmeric, and dried chili and continue cooking 1 minute. Stir in the undrained tomatoes and cook 5 minutes more, stirring occasionally, to make a thick sauce.

4   Add the garbanzo beans with their liquid, salt, and garam masala, then reduce the heat. Cover and simmer 10 minutes.

5   Stir in the spinach, then increase the heat and bring the mixture to a boil. Cook 5 minutes more until the spinach is tender and the liquid almost evaporated. Check the seasonings. Serve with rice or warm bread.

Cook's Tip
You may purchase garam masala or, to make your own, combine 1 tablespoon ground cumin, 1 tablespoon ground coriander, 2 teaspoons black pepper, 2 teaspoons ground cardamom, 1 teaspoon ground cloves, and 1 teaspoon ground cinnamon. Store in an airtight container. Makes ¼ cup.

Nutrition facts per serving: 233 calories, 13 g total fat (1 g saturated fat), 0 mg cholesterol, 1,064 mg sodium, 25 g carbohydrate, 7 g fiber, 7 g protein. **Daily Values:** 42% vitamin A, 33% vitamin C, 12% calcium, 37% iron.

PASTA WITH GARBANZO BEANS AND SAGE

LOW-FAT

Time to make: about 5 minutes
Time to cook: 25 minutes

Serves 2

½ onion

1 garlic clove

1 celery stalk

1 tablespoon olive oil

1 7½-ounce can tomatoes (undrained), chopped

½ tablespoon chopped fresh sage

Salt and freshly ground black pepper

1 cup rinsed and drained canned garbanzo beans

6 ounces dried medium pasta shells or corkscrew pasta

Extra virgin olive oil

Grated Parmesan cheese

This is another variation on a classic tomato sauce for pasta. The addition of garbanzo beans and sage turns this into a hearty, filling dish that will satisfy even the hungriest meat-eater. Get out your best extra virgin olive oil—a nice green pungent one is ideal—to add a final touch of flavor.

1 To prepare the vegetables, finely chop the onion, garlic, and celery.
2 Heat the oil in a medium saucepan over low heat. Add the onion, garlic, and celery and cook 3 minutes, stirring occasionally, until softened but not browned.
3 Add the undrained tomatoes, sage, salt, and pepper and turn up the heat. Bring to a boil, then lower the heat and simmer 15 minutes until you have a thick sauce. Add the garbanzo beans to the tomato mixture. Simmer 5 minutes more.
4 Meanwhile, bring a large saucepan of water to a boil over high heat. Add the pasta and cook 10 to 12 minutes until it is just tender. Drain well.
5 Transfer the hot pasta to a serving bowl and immediately stir in the hot sauce. Serve immediately, drizzled with extra virgin olive oil and sprinkled with Parmesan cheese.

Cook's Tip
If you can't find fresh sage, I recommend you substitute fresh rosemary rather than use dried sage, which can be rather musty and overpowering.

Nutrition facts per serving: 468 calories, 10 g total fat (1 g saturated fat), 0 mg cholesterol, 690 mg sodium, 80 g carbohydrate, 7 g fiber, 16 g protein.
Daily Values: 7% vitamin A, 44% vitamin C, 8% calcium, 41% iron.

Pasta dishes

There can be no cooking process in the world much simpler than cooking pasta, so much so that it now appears regularly in some form or other at mealtimes in every household. Not surprisingly, this is the chapter I cook from the most. This collection of recipes shows the infinite variety of ways saucing, stir-frying, and baking can transform a basic starch into so many satisfying dishes.

SPAGHETTI WITH ZUCCHINI, GARLIC, AND CHILI

Time to make: about 5 minutes
Time to cook: 10 to 12 minutes

Serves 3

6 ounces dried spaghetti

3 small zucchini

2 garlic cloves

1 or 2 dried red chili peppers

3 tablespoons olive oil

**Salt and freshly ground
    black pepper**

Freshly grated Parmesan cheese

This dish is the creation of my sister-in-law, Debbie, who cooks it using zucchini picked fresh from her vegetable garden. If you are not as lucky as she, choose small zucchini with no blemishes and use them as soon as possible after buying.

1 Bring a large saucepan of water to a boil over high heat. Add the spaghetti and cook 10 to 12 minutes until it is just tender. Drain well.

2 Meanwhile, cut the zucchini into quarters lengthwise, then slice thinly. Slice the garlic and chop the chili peppers.

3 Heat the oil in a skillet over medium heat. Add the garlic and fry briskly 1 minute, stirring occasionally, until it is lightly browned. Remove garlic from the pan with a slotted spoon and set aside.

4 Add the zucchini and chili peppers to the pan and fry 3 to 5 minutes, stirring occasionally, until lightly browned but still crisp-tender. Add salt and pepper; return the garlic to the pan.

5 Transfer the drained spaghetti to a serving dish. Top with zucchini and toss to combine. Serve immediately with grated Parmesan cheese.

Cook's Tips

A half-Sicilian friend once gave me some basic tips for cooking pasta, which give excellent results. Use a very large pan of water so that the pasta can move around as the water boils; only stir once when you add the pasta, then keep the water at a steady simmer so the pasta does not stick together. When the pasta is just *al dente*—still has a slightly firm bite—remove the pan from the heat. Run cold water into the pan before draining. This stops the pasta from cooking and prevents sticking.

Nutrition facts per serving: 382 calories, 16 g total fat (2 g saturated fat), 3 mg cholesterol, 109 mg sodium, 50 g carbohydrate, 2 g fiber, 10 g protein.
Daily Values: 7% vitamin A, 8% vitamin C, 5% calcium, 18% iron.

Adding the zucchini, garlic, and chili peppers to the freshly cooked spaghetti

TAGLIATELLE WITH BROILED PEPPER AND EGGPLANT

Time to make: about 5 minutes
Time to cook: 15 minutes

Serves 3

1 red pepper

1 small eggplant

1 onion

1 garlic clove

2 tablespoons extra virgin olive oil

5 ounces dried tagliatelle

2 teaspoons balsamic vinegar

Salt and freshly ground black pepper

3 ounces mozzarella cheese

4 fresh basil leaves

Freshly grated Parmesan

Broiling eggplant brings out its intense smoky flavor without adding too much fat, and it's a technique I use a lot, as I'm a devoted eggplant fan. Properly treated, the flesh has a rich, distinctive quality that turns most people into instant fanatics. This dish is also excellent served at room temperature as a salad.

1   Preheat the broiler to medium. To prepare the vegetables, halve, core, and seed the pepper. Cut the eggplant in half lengthwise and quarter the onion. Mince the garlic.
2   Arrange the pepper, eggplant halves, and onion quarters on the broiler pan. Brush with 1 tablespoon of the olive oil and broil 15 minutes, turning them over occasionally, until they are browned all over and tender.
3   Meanwhile, bring a large pan of water to a boil over high heat. Add the pasta and cook about 10 minutes until it is just tender.
4   Slice the broiled pepper, eggplant, and onion, then put them in a bowl with the remaining 1 tablespoon olive oil. Add the vinegar, garlic, salt, and pepper and toss well together.
5   Drain and cube the mozzarella and shred the basil leaves.
6   Drain the pasta and immediately put it in a large serving dish. Add the dressed vegetables, mozzarella cheese, and basil and toss well together. Serve immediately with Parmesan cheese.

Nutrition facts per serving: 401 calories, 16 g total fat (4 g saturated fat), 19 mg cholesterol, 238 mg sodium, 49 g carbohydrate, 4 g fiber, 17 g protein.
Daily Values: 25% vitamin A, 79% vitamin C, 21% calcium, 19% iron.

PASTA SHELLS WITH SPROUTS

Time to make: about 2 minutes
Time to cook: 10 to 12 minutes

Serves 3

6 ounces dried pasta shells

1 garlic clove

2 ounces goat cheese

2 tablespoons olive oil

2 tablespoons black olive paste (see note, page 45)

1 cup mixed seeds or bean sprouts, such as mung bean, alfalfa, soybean, or radish

Salt and freshly ground black pepper

Sprouted seeds and beans make a valuable addition to a vegetarian diet, as they are rich sources of protein, fiber, vitamins, and minerals. I add them to salads and sandwiches but have to admit that I buy mine in bags from supermarkets, despite repeated assurances from my colleagues that these foods are simple to grow at home.

1 Bring a large saucepan of water to a boil over high heat. Add the pasta and cook 10 to 12 minutes until it is just tender. Drain well and transfer to a serving bowl.
2 Meanwhile, mince the garlic and dice the goat cheese.
3 While the pasta is still cooking, heat the oil in a small skillet over medium heat. Add the garlic and cook 1 minute until lightly browned.
4 Add the cooked garlic and oil to the hot pasta with the olive paste, goat cheese, and sprouts. Season well and toss gently together until well mixed. Serve immediately.

Cook's Tip
Look for jars of olive paste in larger supermarkets and specialty food stores. Different varieties are available and they are wonderful for adding to pasta as in this recipe, spreading on good bread for quick snacks or predinner nibbles, or stirring into rice or vegetable stews.

Nutrition facts per serving: 384 calories, 17 g total fat (4 g saturated fat), 17 mg cholesterol, 197 mg sodium, 47 g carbohydrate, 2 g fiber, 12 g protein.
Daily Values: 3% vitamin A, 5% vitamin C, 3% calcium, 19% iron.

CREAMY PASTA WITH BROILED RED PEPPERS AND PEAS

Time to make: about 15 minutes
Time to cook: 10 to 12 minutes

Serves 3

1 large red bell pepper

⅓ cup frozen peas

6 ounces dried pasta, such as macaroni or fusilli

1 tablespoon olive oil

2 ounces soft cheese with herbs and garlic

2 tablespoons crème fraîche (see Note, page 87)

Salt and freshly ground black pepper

2 tablespoons shredded fresh basil

Freshly grated Parmesan cheese

Sweet broiled peppers and peas complement each other so well in this dish. Pick a soft cheese such as Boursin, which is made without rennet, and serve with a mixed leaf salad.

1 Preheat the broiler to high. Place the whole pepper on the broiler pan and broil about 5 minutes, turning occasionally, until the skin is blackened on all sides. Place the pepper in a plastic bag for 2 minutes to loosen the skin.

2 Meanwhile, cook the peas in a saucepan of boiling water 2 minutes until just tender. Drain well, rinse under cold water and drain again.

3 Halve, core, and seed the pepper, then peel off the skin. Cut the flesh into 1-inch strips.

4 Bring a large saucepan of water to a boil over high heat. Add the pasta and cook 10 to 12 minutes until it is just tender. Drain well.

5 While the pasta is cooking, heat the olive oil in a large skillet over medium heat. Add the pepper strips and cook for 1 minute, stirring occasionally, then stir in the soft cheese and crème fraîche and continue stirring to make a smooth, creamy sauce. Add the peas, salt, and pepper, then turn up the heat and bring to a boil.

6 Add the pasta and the shredded basil and toss together well to coat the pasta in the sauce. Transfer to warmed dishes and serve with grated Parmesan cheese.

Nutrition facts per serving: 390 calories, 16 g total fat (6 g saturated fat), 29 mg cholesterol, 223 mg sodium, 50 g carbohydrate, 1 g fiber, 11 g protein.
Daily Values: 31% vitamin A, 92% vitamin C, 7% calcium, 17% iron.

Creamy Pasta with Broiled Red Peppers and Peas

FUSILLI WITH ROQUEFORT AND WALNUTS

Time to make: about 5 minutes
Time to cook: 10 to 12 minutes

Serves 3

6 ounces dried fusilli

3 ounces Roquefort cheese

¼ cup walnut pieces

2 tablespoons sweet white wine or white port

2 tablespoons crème fraîche (see Note, page 87)

Salt and freshly ground black pepper

Chopped fresh flat-leaf parsley, to garnish

You can use any creamy blue cheese for this richly flavored pasta dish, but I confess to a passion for the most expensive, Roquefort. Still, a little of it goes a long way and its distinctive salty tang makes all the difference in this recipe.

As I always have to have some form of vegetable with my food (fruit will do at breakfast!), I serve this with steamed broccoli or a spinach salad.

1 Bring a large saucepan of water to a boil over high heat. Add the pasta and cook 10 to 12 minutes until it is just tender. Drain well and transfer to a serving bowl.

2 Meanwhile, dice the Roquefort cheese and finely chop the walnut pieces.

3 While the pasta is still cooking, put the wine and crème fraîche in a small pan and heat until it is just boiling. Lower the heat, stir in the Roquefort cheese and continue stirring until the cheese melts and the sauce is the consistency of light cream. Season to taste with salt and pepper.

4 Stir the walnuts into the sauce, then pour it over the hot pasta and toss together gently until all the pasta is well coated. Sprinkle the parsley over the top and serve immediately.

Cook's Tip

I nearly always use dried pasta and keep a selection of shapes on hand. To get the best shape for the sauce, use the following guide: the thinner the sauce, the longer the pasta; use short, stubby shapes for thicker, chunkier sauces.

Nutrition facts per serving: 433 calories, 18 g total fat (8 g saturated fat), 30 mg cholesterol, 449 mg sodium, 49 g carbohydrate, 1 g fiber, 15 g protein.
Daily Values: 10% vitamin A, 3% vitamin C, 15% calcium, 17% iron.

WARM PASTA AND PESTO SALAD

Time to make: about 10 minutes,
 plus cooling
Time to cook: 10 to 12 minutes

Serves 3

6 ounces medium shell
 macaroni

1 to 2 tablespoons purchased
 pesto sauce

1 tablespoon olive oil

2 plum tomatoes

2 green onions

2 ounces feta cheese

1 tablespoon pine nuts,
 optional

8 pitted black olives

Salt and freshly ground
 black pepper

I keep a tub of ready-made pesto permanently in the refrigerator and add it to all kinds of dishes. To pass it off as the real thing, I add extra fresh basil and really good olive oil just before serving.

1 Bring a large saucepan of water to a boil over high heat. Add the pasta and cook 10 to 12 minutes until it is just tender. Drain well and place in a large bowl.
2 Add the pesto and olive oil to the pasta and mix together well. Set aside 15 minutes to cool to room temperature.
3 Meanwhile, prepare the vegetables and cheese. Seed and chop the tomatoes. Chop the green onions. Cube the feta cheese.
4 If you are using the pine nuts, heat a small skillet over high heat. Add the pine nuts and stir-fry until they are golden, then immediately turn them out of the pan to stop the cooking.
5 Add the tomatoes, cheese, green onions, and olives to the pasta and mix together well. Season with salt and pepper and sprinkle with the pine nuts, if you are using. Serve with bread to mop up any extra dressing.

Cook's Tip
Ready-made pesto is now widely available, and the fresh versions are far superior to most pestos sold in jars. If you can't find a type you like, however, make a large batch yourself and freeze it in ice-cube trays. Then you can use a cube at a time as you need it.

Nutrition facts per serving: 384 calories, 16 g total fat (4 g saturated fat), 18 mg cholesterol, 369 mg sodium, 48 g carbohydrate, 1 g fiber, 12 g protein.
Daily Values: 7% vitamin A, 14% vitamin C, 9% calcium, 17% iron.

CHINESE-STYLE NOODLES WITH BROCCOLI AND SESAME

LOW-FAT

Time to make: about 5 minutes
Time to cook: about 15 minutes

Serves 3

½ pound broccoli

1 garlic clove

1-inch piece fresh gingerroot

1 dried red chili

1 cup baby corn

6 ounces Chinese noodles

2 tablespoons tahini paste

1 tablespoon dark soy sauce

1 tablespoon red wine vinegar

1 tablespoon dark brown sugar

1 tablespoon sunflower oil

1 tablespoon sesame seeds

I use Chinese rice noodles in this recipe but tagliatelle works just as well, and I have also made it with egg noodles. This sesame sauce works well with any combination of vegetables, but I particularly like the color and texture combination of broccoli and baby corn.

1 To prepare the vegetables, cut the broccoli into flowerets. Chop the garlic, peel and chop the ginger, and chop the chili.
2 Bring a large saucepan of water to a boil over high heat. Add the broccoli and corn and return the water to a boil, then remove the vegetables from the pan with a slotted spoon and plunge into cold water. Drain and pat dry with paper towels.
3 Add the noodles to the pan of boiling water and cook for 5 minutes or until tender. Drain; rinse under cold water to cool, then drain again.
4 Meanwhile, put the tahini paste, soy sauce, vinegar, and sugar in a bowl and mix together, then set aside.
5 Heat the oil in a wok or large skillet over high heat until almost smoking. Add the garlic, ginger, and chili pepper and stir-fry 30 seconds. Add the broccoli and corn and continue stir-frying for 3 minutes.
6 Add the cooked noodles to the pan along with the tahini mixture; cook and stir for 2 minutes more or until heated through. Sprinkle with sesame seeds and serve immediately.

Cook's Tip
Tahini paste is made from sesame seeds and comes in two versions—dark and light. The only difference is that, in the dark variety, the seeds have been toasted, which intensifies the nutty flavor. If your tahini has oil floating on top, stir it through the paste before using, as the excess oil will affect the texture of the final sauce.

Nutrition facts per serving: 367 calories, 13 g total fat (2 g saturated fat), 49 mg cholesterol, 391 mg sodium, 51 g carbohydrate, 5 g fiber, 13 g protein.
Daily Values: 15% vitamin A, 99% vitamin C, 6% calcium, 26% iron.

Chinese-style Noodles with Broccoli and Sesame

GNOCCHI WITH CREAMED TOMATO AND BASIL SAUCE

Time to make: about 10 minutes
Time to cook: about 20 minutes

Serves 2

4 ounces dried gnocchi (shell-shaped pasta)

Sauce

1 shallot

1 small carrot

1 celery stalk

1 tablespoon sunflower or vegetable oil

1 7½-ounce can tomatoes (undrained), chopped

2 tablespoons chopped fresh basil

Salt and freshly ground black pepper

3 tablespoons whipping cream or half-and-half

Fresh basil leaves, to garnish

Freshly grated Parmesan cheese

This is an immensely useful sauce that I make up in batches (minus the cream) and freeze for use in all kinds of dishes. I serve it on pasta, add vegetables for a stew, or simmer it until it is really thick to use as a topping for pizzas.

1 To prepare the vegetables for the sauce, chop the shallot and finely chop the carrot and celery.

2 Heat the oil in a small saucepan over medium heat. Add the shallot, carrot, and celery and cook 5 minutes until softened.

3 Stir in the undrained tomatoes, basil, salt, and pepper. Bring to a boil, then lower heat and simmer 10 minutes, stirring occasionally, until the liquid has been reduced by half.

4 Place the sauce in a blender or processor and blend or process for 2 minutes until smooth, then return to the pan. Stir in the cream and reheat gently, but *do not allow to boil.* Check the seasonings.

5 Meanwhile, cook the gnocchi according to package directions. Drain pasta thoroughly.

6 To serve, place the gnocchi in a serving dish; pour the sauce over the pasta. Garnish with basil leaves and serve with Parmesan cheese.

Cook's Tip

You can triple or quadruple the sauce and freeze it to keep on hand for a quick meal. To freeze the sauce, omit the cream and let sauce cool completely. Transfer serving-size amounts (1 recipe makes about 1⅓ cups) to a rigid container. Cover and freeze for up to 1 month. To use, slowly thaw the frozen sauce over low heat. Stir in the cream.

Nutrition facts per serving: 398 calories, 16 g total fat (6 g saturated fat), 31 mg cholesterol, 297 mg sodium, 54 g carbohydrate, 3 g fiber, 10 g protein.
Daily Values: 86% vitamin A, 32% vitamin C, 6% calcium, 21% iron.

PASTA SHELLS WITH BLACK OLIVE PASTE

Time to make: 5 minutes
Time to cook: 10 to 12 minutes

Serves 3

6 ounces small dried pasta, such as medium shell, corkscrew, or elbow macaroni (about 2 cups)

¼ cup pine nuts

1 tablespoon black olive paste*

3 tablespoons shredded fresh basil

2 tablespoons olive oil

3 tablespoons grated pecorino, Parmesan, or romano cheese

Salt and freshly ground black pepper

Ready-made olive pastes now appear on many supermarket and delicatessen shelves, but take care when buying them, as they can vary greatly in quality. Look for ones made from only olives, good-quality olive oil, and just a few added herbs; some brands use sunflower oil and all kinds of flavorings and lose flavor intensity as a result.

1 Bring a large saucepan of water to a boil over high heat. Add the pasta and cook 10 to 12 minutes until tender.
2 Meanwhile, place the pine nuts in a small skillet over medium heat and stir-fry for 1 to 2 minutes or until golden.
3 Drain the pasta well and transfer it to a large serving bowl. Add the toasted pine nuts, black olive paste, basil, olive oil, and cheese; toss together gently. Season to taste and serve immediately.

Cook's Tip
To prevent an opened container of olive paste from going bad, always cover the surface with extra olive oil, then cover and store in a cool, dark place.

***Note**
If you can't find black olive paste, you can make your own. Process about 32 pitted ripe olives with a small amount of olive oil (1 teaspoon) until a paste forms. Makes about ¼ cup.

Nutrition facts per serving: 405 calories, 20 g total fat (4 g saturated fat), 5 mg cholesterol, 201 mg sodium, 46 g carbohydrate, 1 g fiber, 13 g protein.
Daily Values: 1% vitamin A, 0% vitamin C, 9% calcium, 23% iron.

STIR-FRIED GREENS WITH TOFU AND NOODLES

Time to make: 5 minutes
Time to cook: 20 to 25 minutes

Serves 2

4 ounces Chinese egg noodles

4 ounces marinated or
    smoked tofu

1 garlic clove

1-inch piece fresh gingerroot

4 green onions

½ pound Chinese cabbage

1 carrot

Vegetable oil for deep-frying

2 tablespoons sunflower oil

3 tablespoons soy sauce

1 tablespoon dark brown sugar

1 tablespoon red wine vinegar

1 tablespoon sesame oil

Tofu can be delicious when treated properly, but many people are put off at the first attempt by the bland taste and somewhat flabby texture. I find marinating it and then roasting or deep-frying it makes it far more palatable, or you could try the smoked variety. Be careful with adding salt, though, as smoked tofu can be very salty.

1 Bring a large saucepan of water to a boil over high heat. Add the noodles and cook according to package instructions. Drain; rinse under cold water and drain again, then set aside.
2 Meanwhile, cut the tofu into 2 inch cubes. To prepare the vegetables, mince the garlic. Peel and chop the ginger. Slice the green onions. Shred the cabbage and halve the carrot lengthwise and then slice it.
3 Heat about 2 inches of vegetable oil in a wok or small deep skillet over high heat. Add the tofu cubes in batches and deep-fry 2 to 3 minutes until golden.
4 Remove the cubes from the wok or pan with a slotted spoon and drain well on paper towels.
5 Heat the sunflower oil in the cleaned wok or in a large skillet over high heat. Add the garlic and ginger and stir-fry 1 minute. Add the green onions, cabbage, and carrot and continue stir-frying 5 minutes until the cabbage is wilted.
6 Place the soy sauce in a bowl and stir in the sugar, vinegar, and ¼ cup water.
7 Add the cooked noodles to the wok or skillet and stir-fry for 1 to 2 minutes. Add the soy sauce mixture and continue stir-frying 2 minutes more. Stir in sesame oil; serve immediately.

Nutrition facts per serving: 561 calories, 32 g total fat (4 g saturated fat), 49 mg cholesterol, 1,601 mg sodium, 56 g carbohydrate, 3 g fiber, 15 g protein.
Daily Values: 92% vitamin A, 88% vitamin C, 12% calcium, 47% iron.

Stir-fried Greens with Tofu and Noodles

RICE NOODLES WITH COCONUT AND THAI SPICES

Time to make: about 5 minutes
Time to cook: 20 to 25 minutes

Serves 3

6 ounces medium rice noodles

1 small onion

1 garlic clove

4 ounces marinated or
    smoked tofu

½ cup shiitake or brown
    mushrooms

1 celery stalk

1 tablespoon sunflower oil

1 tablespoon Thai green
    curry paste

⅔ cup vegetable stock or broth

1 cup coconut milk

Chopped fresh cilantro,
    to garnish

Rice noodles are the slightly transparent-looking ones you find in Asian supermarkets. They take very little time to cook and are lighter in texture and less filling than Italian wheat noodles, which makes them so suited to the clean flavors of Thai cooking. My husband enjoys cooking this dish and he starts with fresh lemon grass, chili peppers, and ginger. But during the week I just use a tablespoon of a purchased Thai curry paste. If you enjoy cooking Thai food, there are specialty stores where you can find most, if not all, of the ingredients you need.

1 Bring a large saucepan of water to a boil over high heat. Add the noodles and cook 6 to 10 minutes until tender. Drain and transfer to a bowl of cold water while preparing the rest of the dish—this will keep the noodles from becoming sticky.
2 Meanwhile, slice the onion and chop the garlic. Cube the tofu and slice the mushrooms and celery.
3 Heat the oil in a saucepan over medium heat. Add the onion and garlic and cook 5 minutes, stirring occasionally, until the onion slices are golden. Stir in the curry paste and cook 3 minutes more, stirring constantly. Stir in the stock, reduce the heat and simmer 5 minutes.
4 Stir in the coconut milk. Increase the heat and bring to a boil; stir in the tofu, mushrooms, and the drained noodles. Heat through. To serve, sprinkle with the sliced celery and chopped cilantro.

Nutrition facts per serving: 572 calories, 29 g total fat (17 g saturated fat), 0 mg cholesterol, 563 mg sodium, 63 g carbohydrate, 3 g fiber, 14 g protein.
Daily Values: 5% vitamin A, 5% vitamin C, 9% calcium, 40% iron.

TAGLIATELLE WITH ASPARAGUS AND DRIED TOMATOES

Time to make: 5 minutes
Time to cook: 10 minutes

Serves 3

6 ounces fresh tagliatelle

1 cup asparagus

2 dried tomatoes in oil, drained

1 tablespoon walnut or olive oil

¼ cup dry white wine

**Salt and freshly ground
    black pepper**

2 egg yolks

¼ cup whipping cream

**¼ cup freshly grated
    Parmesan cheese**

This recipe sounds expensive, but isn't. Asparagus is available just about all year around now, although I prefer to wait until it's in season to really enjoy asparagus at its best. Dried tomatoes, despite being saddled with a very trendy reputation, are actually tasty and a welcome addition to any kitchen. Use the ones preserved in oil for this dish, as they are ready to use and don't need presoaking.

1   Bring a large saucepan of water to a boil over high heat. Add the pasta and cook 5 minutes until just tender.
2   While the pasta is cooking, bring another pan of water to a boil. Snap off and discard woody bases from fresh asparagus. Add the asparagus and blanch for 1 minute. Immediately drain and rinse the asparagus under cold water, then drain again. Pat dry with paper towels.
3   Meanwhile, finely chop the dried tomatoes. Heat the walnut or olive oil in a large saucepan over medium heat. Add the asparagus and dried tomatoes. Fry for 2 minutes, stirring occasionally. Stir in the wine, salt, and pepper. Reduce the heat and simmer until the wine reduces by half.
4   Place egg yolks in a bowl; whisk in cream and Parmesan cheese. Add drained pasta to the asparagus; stir to combine. Stir in the cream-and-egg mixture; continue stirring over low heat until sauce just thickens. Check seasonings. Serve immediately.

Cook's Tip
Walnut oil adds a distinctive flavor to this dish. I keep a bottle for adding to dressings and for use in breadmaking. It's particularly good in tea breads. Buy it at supermarkets or delicatessens and store it in a dark, cool place.

Nutrition facts per serving: 444 calories, 19 g total fat (6 g saturated fat), 176 mg cholesterol, 180 mg sodium, 50 g carbohydrate, 1 g fiber, 15 g protein.
Daily Values: 35% vitamin A, 27% vitamin C, 11% calcium, 19% iron.

Vegetable dishes and salads

For many years now there has been an enormous increase in the variety of fresh fruits and vegetables available. When cooking from this chapter, however, I hope you choose recipes that use ingredients that are in season. Not only are the fruits and vegetables likely to be at their peak, but they will taste better, too.

BAKED MUSHROOMS WITH GOAT CHEESE

Time to make: about 5 minutes
Time to cook: 15 minutes

Serves 4

4 large fresh mushrooms, such as portobello

2 teaspoons black olive paste (see Note, page 45)

4 thin slices goat cheese, about 4 ounces total

1 tablespoon pine nuts

2 tablespoons olive oil

Salt and freshly ground black pepper

2 or 3 fresh basil leaves

On the rare occasions that I have an evening alone, I tend to opt out and just have a boiled egg. While writing this book, however, I've felt more inspired to cook something special just for myself, but the requirements of such a dish are these: practically no preparation and ingredients that happen to be in the refrigerator. On one particular night some large mushrooms and goat cheese produced this recipe, which was so good I promptly cooked it for friends the following night as a starter. Warm bread and green beans are all you need to accompany the meal.

1 Preheat the oven to 400°F. To prepare the mushrooms, remove the stems.

2 Spread the dark inside of the mushroom caps with olive paste. Place on an oiled baking sheet.

3 Arrange a slice of goat cheese on each mushroom; sprinkle with pine nuts and drizzle with olive oil. Season with salt and pepper.

4 Bake the mushrooms 15 minutes until the cheese is melted and golden.

5 Meanwhile, shred the basil leaves. Sprinkle basil over the mushrooms and serve.

Cook's Tip

For this quick dish, choose a goat cheese with a rind and a diameter similar to that of the mushrooms. It should sit neatly within each mushroom's cap.

Nutrition facts per serving: 190 calories, 17 g total fat (5 g saturated fat), 25 mg cholesterol, 210 mg sodium, 5 g carbohydrate, 1 g fiber, 8 g protein.
Daily Values: 4% vitamin A, 6% vitamin C, 3% calcium, 13% iron.

Ready to serve Baked Mushrooms with Goat Cheese

SPICED VEGETABLE TORTILLA ROLL-UPS

LOW-FAT

Time to make: 10 to 15 minutes
Time to cook: 10 to 15 minutes

Serves 4

4 ounces whole tiny new potatoes

2 teaspoons sunflower oil

½ small onion, sliced

½ teaspoon grated fresh gingerroot

¼ fresh green chili pepper (such as Anaheim), seeded and chopped (about 3 tablespoons)

½ teaspoon cumin seeds

½ teaspoon garam masala (an Indian spice mix), see Cook's Tip, page 32

2 teaspoons lemon juice

Salt

1 cup frozen mixed vegetables, thawed

1 small tomato, chopped

8 flour tortillas

In the interest of time, tortillas are used in this recipe, although thin pancakes or crepes make it more special. If you have the time, you can make crepes instead (see Cook's Tip, below). Make them ahead of time, if you like, placing the cooled crepes between layers of waxed paper and freezing them. Let crepes thaw at room temperature for one hour before using.

1 Bring a large saucepan of water to a boil over high heat. Add the potatoes and cook 10 minutes until tender.
2 Drain the potatoes thoroughly, then cut them into cubes. Set aside while you prepare the rest of the filling.
3 Heat the oil in a saucepan over medium heat. Add the onion, ginger, chili pepper, and cumin seeds and cook 3 minutes, stirring occasionally, until the onion is softened.
4 Stir in the garam masala, lemon juice, and salt to taste. Cook and stir 30 seconds more. Stir in the potatoes, vegetables, and tomato. Cook and stir for 5 minutes.
5 Wrap tortillas in foil and heat in a 350° oven for 5 minutes.
6 To serve, divide the vegetable mixture among the warm tortillas or crepes; roll up and serve.

Cook's Tip
To make crepes, in a medium bowl beat ¾ cups milk, ½ cup all-purpose flour, 1 egg, 2 teaspoons cooking oil, and a dash of salt until combined. Heat a lightly greased 6-inch skillet. Remove from heat. Spoon *2 tablespoons* of the batter into the skillet; lift and tilt the skillet to spread batter. Return to heat; brown on one side only. Invert pan over paper towels; remove crepe. Repeat with remaining batter, greasing skillet occasionally. Makes 9 crepes.

Nutrition facts per serving: 302 calories, 7 g total fat (1 g saturated fat), 0 mg cholesterol, 385 mg sodium, 52 g carbohydrate, 1 g fiber, 8 g protein.
Daily Values: 16% vitamin A, 30% vitamin C, 9% calcium, 24% iron.

SUMMER VEGETABLE BAKE

Time to make: about 5 minutes
Time to cook: about 25 minutes

Serves 2

3 small zucchini

8 cherry tomatoes

1 small eggplant

1 garlic clove

3 tablespoons extra virgin olive oil

Salt and freshly ground black pepper

¾ cup fresh bread crumbs

3 tablespoons chopped fresh flat-leaf parsley

When fresh vegetables are at their peak, they need little enhancement, as the wonderful flavors work together to make a satisfying dish on their own. Last summer I grew a single zucchini plant and the results were used to great effect in this simple recipe. If you add a tumbling tomato plant to your patio display, you can have the tomatoes freshly picked as well.

1 Preheat the oven to 400°F. To prepare the vegetables, cut the zucchini in half and then into 1 inch slices, halve the tomatoes, and halve and slice the eggplant. Chop the garlic.
2 Place the zucchini, tomatoes, and eggplant together in a bowl, then add the oil, salt, and pepper and toss to coat the vegetables in the oil. Arrange in an oiled casserole dish large enough to hold all of the vegetables in a single layer.
3 Bake, basting with oil and juices, until the vegetables are golden, about 20 minutes.
4 Meanwhile, put the crumbs in a small bowl and stir in the garlic and parsley.
5 Spoon the mixture over the vegetable juices to soak up the juices, then return the dish to the oven 5 minutes more or until golden. Serve with crusty bread to mop up any juices.

Cook's Tip
Add fresh basil and mozzarella slices to make this a heartier supper dish. Simply slice 3 ounces mozzarella cheese and tuck the slices between the vegetables. Add a couple of tablespoons of chopped fresh basil to the topping and continue as above.

Nutrition facts per serving: 313 calories, 22 g total fat (3 g saturated fat), 0 mg cholesterol, 174 mg sodium, 29 g carbohydrate, 8 g fiber, 5 g protein.
Daily Values: 13% vitamin A, 56% vitamin C, 5% calcium, 16% iron.

BRAISED EGGPLANT WITH THAI SPICES

LOW-FAT

Time to make: about 5 minutes
Time to cook: about 25 minutes

Serves 2

| 8 ounces eggplant |
| 1 small onion |
| 1 garlic clove |
| ½-inch piece fresh gingerroot |
| 2 teaspoons sunflower oil |
| 1 to 2 teaspoons red curry paste |
| 1 to 2 tablespoons fresh lime juice |
| 1 tablespoon dark brown sugar |
| ½ teaspoon black bean sauce |
| Salt |
| 8 fresh basil leaves (use Thai basil if you can get it) |
| Finely shredded lime rind, to garnish |

As anyone who has read through this book will have realized, eggplant (along with broiled red peppers) makes a very regular appearance in the Gwynn household in one form or other. This recipe must be one of my favorites, as the sweet-and-sour Thai sauce really complements both the texture and smoky taste of the vegetable. What's more, it is incredibly simple to prepare, cooks in no time, and is just as good cold. I like to eat this with Thai fragrant rice.

1   To prepare the vegetables, cube the eggplant, slice the onion, and mince the garlic. Chop the ginger.
2   Heat the oil in a wok or large skillet over medium heat. Add the onion, garlic, and ginger and stir-fry 3 minutes until just beginning to brown.
3   Stir in the curry paste and cook 1 minute. Add the eggplant cubes and stir-fry about 3 minutes until they are lightly browned.
4   Stir in the lime juice, sugar, black bean sauce, salt to taste, and 1¼ cups cold water and bring to a boil, stirring often. Reduce heat; cover and simmer 15 minutes until the eggplant is tender.
5   Remove the lid and continue simmering the mixture until the liquid is reduced and the sauce is thick and syrupy. Stir in the basil, garnish, and serve immediately.

Cook's Tips

Red curry paste is available in Asian supermarkets and specialty stores. It can be very hot so use it sparingly if it's a brand you have not tried before.

Thai basil, also called holy basil, is particularly aromatic and stands up to the strong flavors used here. You will find it in Asian supermarkets.

Nutrition facts per serving: 181 calories, 12 g total fat (1 g saturated fat), 0 mg cholesterol, 78 mg sodium, 19 g carbohydrate, 4 g fiber, 2 g protein.
Daily Values: 5% vitamin A, 10% vitamin C, 5% calcium, 20% iron.

Braised Eggplant with Thai Spices served with rice

SWEET POTATO HASH

Time to make: about 5 minutes
Time to cook: about 20 minutes,
  plus broiling

Serves 2

6 ounces sweet potato

6 ounces potato

1 small leek

½ small onion

1 tablespoon olive oil

Dash ground ginger

**1 tablespoon chopped fresh
  flat-leaf parsley**

**Salt and freshly ground
  black pepper**

2 teaspoons olive oil

1 ounce Gruyère cheese

I really started buying sweet potatoes on a regular basis when
I discovered them as the perfect starchy vegetable for my two
toddler daughters, who back then preferred them to ordinary
potatoes. The girls still enjoy sweet potatoes, but in dishes like
this hash rather than pureed. Try to get the pink-fleshed potatoes
if you can—they look far more attractive than the slightly green-
fleshed ones, which go gray when cooked.

1 Bring 2 saucepans of water to a boil over high heat. While
they are heating, cube both kinds of potatoes. Add all potatoes to
boiling water and cook 10 minutes until tender. Drain thoroughly,
then place in a large mixing bowl and mash potatoes together.
2 Meanwhile, thinly slice the leek, rinse in cold water and drain
thoroughly. Thinly slice the onion.
3 Heat the 1 tablespoon of oil in an oven-safe skillet over
medium heat. Add the leek and onion and cook 5 minutes until
softened and lightly browned. Add to the potatoes. Stir in the
ginger, parsley, salt, and pepper. Mix well.
4 Heat the remaining 2 teaspoons of oil in the cleaned skillet
over medium heat until very hot. Add the potato mixture and fry
for 5 minutes until heated through and beginning to brown.
Flatten the potato into a pancake with the back of the spoon and
cook until the base is golden and crisp.
5 Meanwhile, preheat the broiler and grate the cheese. Sprinkle
cheese on top of the hash; broil 3 to 4 minutes until bubbly. Cut
into wedges and serve immediately with a green vegetable.

Cook's Tip
Shredded cabbage makes a good addition to this dish; however,
when I do add it, I replace the ground ginger with caraway seeds.

Nutrition facts per serving: 323 calories, 15 g total fat (4 g saturated fat),
15 mg cholesterol, 136 mg sodium, 41 g carbohydrate, 5 g fiber, 8 g protein.
Daily Values: 151% vitamin A, 56% vitamin C, 16% calcium, 17% iron.

MUSHROOM AND COCONUT CURRY

Time to make: about 10 minutes
Time to cook: about 20 minutes

Serves 2

2 cups brown or button mushrooms

1 small onion

½ clove garlic

1 tablespoon vegetable oil

½ teaspoon chopped fresh gingerroot

¼ teaspoon ground cumin

½ teaspoon ground coriander

Dash turmeric

Dash ground red pepper

1 to 2 tablespoons coconut milk

3 tablespoons yogurt

½ teaspoon salt

¼ teaspoon garam masala (an Indian spice mix), see Cook's Tip, page 32

½ tablespoon lemon juice

Hot cooked rice

Apparently mushrooms aren't traditionally used in Indian cookery, so mushroom curries are relative newcomers to the scene. About five years ago I came across a particularly tasty mushroom curry subtly flavored with coconut; that inspired this recipe, which makes a wonderful quick supper served with basmati rice and a lentil pilaf.

1 To prepare the vegetables, halve the mushrooms and finely chop the onion and garlic.
2 Heat the oil in a saucepan over low heat. Add the garlic, ginger, and onion. Cook 5 minutes, stirring occasionally, until softened.
3 Stir in the cumin, coriander, turmeric, and red pepper. Cook for 1 minute. Add the mushrooms; cover and cook 10 minutes until the mushrooms are softened, stirring occasionally.
4 Stir the coconut milk into the mushrooms. Stir in the yogurt, salt, and garam masala. Simmer, uncovered, 2 minutes until the sauce is the consistency of thick cream. (*Do not boil.*)
5 Stir in the lemon juice. Serve immediately over hot rice.

Nutrition facts per serving: 131 calories, 10 g total fat (3 g saturated fat), 1 mg cholesterol, 553 mg sodium, 9 g carbohydrate, 1 g fiber, 4 g protein.
Daily Values: 0% vitamin A, 10% vitamin C, 5% calcium, 13% iron.

BABY SPINACH & LIMA BEAN SALAD WITH GARLIC CROUTONS

Time to make: about 10 minutes
Time to cook: 5 to 8 minutes

Serves 3

2 pounds fresh lima beans

6 green onions

4 ounces feta cheese

About 6 ounces fresh
   baby spinach

1 tablespoon chopped fresh mint

1 tablespoon white wine
   vinegar

3 tablespoons extra virgin
   olive oil

Salt and freshly ground pepper

Croutons

1 large slice white country bread

1 garlic clove

2 tablespoons olive oil

Lima beans are one of those vegetables which really bring home the pleasures of eating with the seasons. I think they are only really worth eating fresh, preferably just picked, as the grayish skin, which coats each bean, becomes tough when the beans get too large or are frozen. Fresh picked, blanched in boiling water, and tossed in a salad, they are a true taste of summer for me. Look for them from June through September.

1   To prepare the vegetables, shell the lima beans (you should have about ½ pound limas). Chop the green onions. Cube the feta cheese.

2   Bring a saucepan of water to a boil over high heat. Add the beans and cook 2 minutes until just tender. Drain, rinse under cold water and drain again. Pat dry with paper towels.

3   Place the beans in a salad bowl with the spinach, green onions, and feta cheese.

4   To make a dressing, put the mint, vinegar, oil, salt, and pepper in a small bowl and whisk until well combined.

5   To prepare the croutons, cut the bread into large cubes and mince the garlic. Heat the oil in a small skillet over medium heat. Add the bread cubes and garlic and stir-fry until they are golden. Remove the croutons from the pan with a slotted spoon and drain on paper towels. Sprinkle with salt.

6   Add the croutons to the salad. Add the dressing; toss gently to coat ingredients. Serve immediately with warm bread.

Cook's Tip
If using frozen beans, blanch them, then slip off the gray skins before adding to the salad.

Nutrition facts per serving: 438 calories, 31 g total fat (9 g saturated fat), 33 mg cholesterol, 620 mg sodium, 28 g carbohydrate, 7 g fiber, 13 g protein.
Daily Values: 47% vitamin A, 24% vitamin C, 24% calcium, 29% iron.

Baby Spinach & Lima Bean Salad
with Garlic Croutons

GADO-GADO

Time to make: about 10 minutes
Time to cook: about 15 minutes

Serves 3

6 ounces tiny new potatoes, quartered

1 carrot (½ cup)

6 ounces green beans (1⅓ cups)

6 ounces white cabbage (2 cups shredded)

¼ of a cucumber (½ cup)

2 cups fresh bean sprouts

Peanut Sauce

1 garlic clove

1 teaspoon sunflower oil

¼ cup crunchy peanut butter

1 tablespoon soy sauce

1 teaspoon dark brown sugar

1 tablespoon lemon juice

½ teaspoon chili paste

¼ cup coconut milk

This is my version of the increasingly popular Indonesian vegetable salad. The sauce also goes well with vegetable kabobs, served satay style.

1 Bring 2 saucepans of water to a boil over high heat. Add the potatoes to one and cook 10 minutes until tender. Drain, rinse under cool water and drain again. Pat dry with paper towels.

2 Meanwhile, peel and cut the carrot into matchsticks, halve the green beans crosswise, shred the cabbage, and cut the cucumber into matchsticks.

3 Add the carrot and green beans to the second saucepan, return to a boil and cook for 3 minutes, adding the cabbage for the last minute—the vegetables should still be crisp. Drain, rinse in a bowl of cold water and drain again. Pat dry with paper towels.

4 Place the cooked vegetables in a large salad bowl, add the bean sprouts and cucumber and gently toss together.

5 To prepare the sauce, mince the garlic. Heat the oil in a small pan over medium heat. Add the garlic and cook 30 seconds or until golden. Stir in the peanut butter and ¼ cup cold water until well blended.

6 Remove pan from heat; stir in the soy sauce, sugar, lemon juice, and chili paste. Return the pan to the heat and simmer, stirring, to make a smooth sauce.

7 Stir in the coconut milk; heat through and pour over the salad. Toss gently and serve.

Nutrition facts per serving: 317 calories, 18 g total fat (6 g saturated fat), 0 mg cholesterol, 496 mg sodium, 33 g carbohydrate, 6 g fiber, 11 g protein.
Daily Values: 56% vitamin A, 63% vitamin C, 7% calcium, 22% iron.

CELERIAC AND CARROT REMOULADE

Time to make: 10 to 15 minutes

Serves 3

**6 ounces celeriac
(¾ cup grated)**

6 ounces carrot (¾ cup grated)

2 teaspoons capers

1 tablespoon lemon juice

**Chopped flat-leaf parsley,
to garnish**

Mustard Mayonnaise

1 small egg yolk*

1 teaspoon Dijon-style mustard

**Salt and freshly ground black
pepper**

⅓ cup olive oil

1 tablespoon lemon juice

Milk

My parents-in-law live in the north of France and, when we visit them, my husband's mother stocks up on celeriac remoulade from her local delicatessen or supermarket. This simple combination of root vegetables with a mustard-flavored mayonnaise is great as a starter on picnics, and is a family favorite. Because it is not widely available in this country and I have to make it, I add carrot for sweetness and a few capers for extra bite.

1 To prepare the vegetables, peel and coarsely grate the celeriac and carrot or cut them into very thin matchsticks.
2 Place the celeriac and carrot in a bowl with the capers and lemon juice and mix well to combine.
3 To make Mustard Mayonnaise, place the egg yolk in a small bowl with the mustard, salt, and pepper and mix together well. Gradually dribble in the olive oil, whisking constantly, until the mixture becomes thick and creamy. Stir in the lemon juice and, if the mayonnaise is too thick, add a little milk to give a coating consistency. Check the seasonings.
4 Pour the mayonnaise over the vegetables and toss gently to coat. Transfer to a serving dish, sprinkle with parsley and serve.

*Note
Young children, older adults, or those who are ill or have an immune system deficiency should avoid eating raw eggs.

Nutrition facts per serving: 270 calories, 26 g total fat (4 g saturated fat), 71 mg cholesterol, 184 mg sodium, 9 g carbohydrate, 3 g fiber, 2 g protein.
Daily Values: 171% vitamin A, 26% vitamin C, 4% calcium, 5% iron.

Rice and grain dishes

Go into any food store these days, head for the rice section and marvel at the selection of rices available in even the smallest store. One of the joys of cooking with various rices is discovering their differences and using them in dishes that make the most of these differences.

POLENTA WITH MUSHROOM SAUCE

Time to make: 10 minutes
Time to cook: about 20 minutes

Serves 2

6 ounces instant polenta

**Salt and freshly ground
black pepper**

**1 tablespoon margarine
or butter**

**¼ cup freshly grated Parmesan
cheese**

Sauce

**½ ounce dried porcini
mushrooms**

1 shallot

**1 cup brown or button
mushrooms**

2 tablespoons olive oil

⅔ cup tomato puree

**2 tablespoons chopped fresh
flat-leaf parsley**

2 tablespoons dry white wine

Polenta is one of those dishes that has become very trendy with the new wave of Mediterranean peasant-style cookery. It can be disappointingly bland but, with cheese and a touch of butter, it makes an excellent dish. I like to allow the cooked polenta to cool until firm, then cut it into slices, and fry or broil the slices to give them a little texture. Served with a richly flavored sauce, such as this one, polenta makes a colorful meal at any time of the year.

1 First prepare the sauce. Place the dried mushrooms in a small bowl, add enough hot water to cover and let soak for 10 minutes.
2 Meanwhile, chop the shallot and slice the brown or button mushrooms. Heat the oil in a saucepan over high heat. Add the shallot and mushrooms and cook 5 minutes, stirring occasionally, until they are softened.
3 Drain the porcini mushrooms, reserving the soaking liquid. Chop the drained mushrooms. Add them to the pan along with the tomato puree, parsley, white wine, and reserved soaking liquid. Season with salt and pepper, reduce the heat to medium and simmer until you have a thick sauce, 10 minutes.
4 For the polenta, place 3 cups cold water in a large pan over high heat and bring to a boil. Add ½ teaspoon salt and pour in the polenta, stirring constantly. Lower the heat and simmer 5 to 8 minutes, stirring constantly until the polenta is thick and coming away from the sides of the pan. Stir in the margarine or butter and cheese.
5 Divide the polenta between individual dishes and top with the mushroom sauce. Serve immediately.

Nutrition facts per serving: 594 calories, 24 g total fat (3 g saturated fat), 10 mg cholesterol, 314 mg sodium, 78 g carbohydrate, 11 g fiber, 16 g protein.
Daily Values: 30% vitamin A, 46% vitamin C, 13% calcium, 23% iron.

*Butter and cheese being added to the
polenta mixture*

VEGETABLE RISOTTO

Time to make: about 5 minutes
Time to cook: about 25 minutes

Serves 2

½ small onion

½ garlic clove

1 small zucchini

½ cup green beans

½ medium eggplant

1 canned pimiento, drained

1 small tomato

1¼ cups vegetable stock
   or broth

2 tablespoons olive oil

¾ cup uncooked arborio rice

2 teaspoons paprika

Salt and freshly ground
   black pepper

Chopped fresh parsley,
   to garnish

This recipe is a family favorite. I find it's a great way to get my children to eat vegetables, such as zucchini, that would be turned down if presented in a more recognizable form. It is, however, a recipe that comes close to overstepping the 30-minute mark, but the preparation involved is quite simple.

1 To prepare the vegetables, chop the onion, garlic, and zucchini. Cut the green beans into short lengths and cube the eggplant. Chop the pimiento and tomato.
2 In a small saucepan bring the stock or broth to boiling. Keep broth hot.
3 Meanwhile, heat the oil in a large saucepan over medium heat. Add the onion and garlic and cook 3 minutes, stirring occasionally, until softened but not browned.
4 Stir in the zucchini, beans, eggplant, and pimiento, increase the heat and continue cooking 5 minutes more, stirring occasionally, until the vegetables are lightly browned.
5 Stir in the tomato, rice, and paprika. Turn down the heat and continue cooking 1 minute. Add the hot stock or broth and the seasonings. Increase the heat and bring to a boil, stirring occasionally.
6 Lower the heat. Cover and simmer 15 to 20 minutes until the rice is just tender. Let the pan stand, covered, about 5 minutes. To serve, fluff the rice with a fork and garnish with chopped parsley.

About Rices
The Italians and Spanish, with their distinctive risottos and paellas, both use similar short-grained rices that produce the creamy texture so prized in these dishes. Valencia rice from Spain is not readily available so I use arborio rice instead. Basmati rice with its fragrant delicate grains is ideal with Indian food; the slightly sticky jasmine rice makes a perfect partner for Thai food.

Nutrition facts per serving: 295 calories, 10 g total fat (1 g saturated fat), 0 mg cholesterol, 443 mg sodium, 49 g carbohydrate, 3 g fiber, 5 g protein.
Daily Values: 15% vitamin A, 30% vitamin C, 3% calcium, 15% iron.

MUSHROOM RICE WITH COCONUT

Time to make: about 5 minutes
Time to cook: about 25 minutes

Serves 3

1 cup uncooked jasmine rice

1 stalk lemon grass

½ to 1 fresh red chili pepper

1½ cups oyster mushrooms

½ cup shiitake mushrooms

1 tablespoon sunflower oil

1 bay leaf

1 cup coconut milk

**Salt and freshly ground
    black pepper**

**Fresh cilantro or basil leaves,
    to garnish**

Jasmine rice has a wonderful, scented aroma when cooked; in fact, it's so delicious I can eat bowls of it on its own. This dish is subtly flavored with coconut, which doesn't overwhelm the delicate rice. Serve it with Braised Eggplant with Thai Spices (see page 54).

1 Rinse the rice in one change of water, then drain. To prepare the vegetables, crush the lemon grass and seed and chop the chili. Slice the oyster and shiitake mushrooms.
2 Heat the oil in a saucepan with a tight-fitting lid over medium heat. Add the lemon grass and chili and cook 1 minute, stirring. Stir in the mushrooms and bay leaf and stir-fry for 5 minutes until the mushrooms are softened.
3 Stir in the coconut milk and add salt and pepper. Bring to a boil, then lower the heat, cover and cook over very low heat for 15 to 20 minutes or until the rice is tender.
4 Remove the lemon grass and bay leaf. To serve, fluff the rice with a fork. If desired, garnish with fresh cilantro or basil.

Cook's Tip
If you are cooking jasmine rice on its own, don't add any salt or pepper as they will mask the delicate flavor of the rice.

Nutrition facts per serving: 496 calories, 27 g total fat (17 g saturated fat), 0 mg cholesterol, 60 mg sodium, 56 g carbohydrate, 1 g fiber, 8 g protein.
Daily Values: 0% vitamin A, 16% vitamin C, 3% calcium, 31% iron.

CURRIED RICE SALAD WITH MANGO

LOW-FAT

Time to make: 10 to 15 minutes
Time to cook: 25 minutes

Serves 3

1 cup uncooked quick-cooking brown rice

1 small ripe mango

6 green onions

2 tablespoons pumpkin seeds

¼ cup roasted cashews

Fresh cilantro sprigs and lime wedges, to garnish

Dressing

1 teaspoon mild curry paste

1½ teaspoons finely grated lime peel

1 lime

3 tablespoons sunflower oil

2 tablespoons chopped fresh cilantro

Salt and freshly ground black pepper

I lived in the South Pacific for 18 months and had the luxury of a mango tree in my garden. Freshly picked, the fruit has a fragrance and aroma that store-bought fruit cannot hope to match. The locals used to prepare a wonderful mango or papaya salad with curry spices in the dressing.

1 Bring a large saucepan of water to a boil over high heat. Add the rice and simmer 25 minutes until it is just tender. Drain and rinse under cold water to cool, then drain again. Pat dry with paper towels.

2 While the rice is cooking, cut the mango flesh away from the pit, holding it over a bowl to catch any juices, then peel and cut into cubes. Place the cubed mango into a large bowl.

3 Chop the green onions, then add them to the bowl along with the pumpkin seeds and cashews.

4 To make the dressing, put the curry paste into a small bowl. Add the lime peel and squeeze in the juice. Whisk in the oil, chopped cilantro, salt, and pepper.

5 Add the drained rice to the mango mixture, pour the dressing over the salad, and toss until completely combined. To serve, transfer to a serving dish and garnish with fresh cilantro and lime wedges.

Cook's Tip
Always use a curry paste instead of dry spices when you are making a dressing or recipe that isn't going to be fried. The ingredients in a paste have already been cooked together a little, so the flavor is developed and not raw tasting.

Nutrition facts per serving: 215 calories, 14 g total fat (2 g saturated fat), 0 mg cholesterol, 35 mg sodium, 23 g carbohydrate, 3 g fiber, 3 g protein.
Daily Values: 17% vitamin A, 26% vitamin C, 1% calcium, 7% iron.

Curried Rice Salad with Mango served with a minty yogurt raita

ROASTED BULGUR WHEAT WITH MINTED DRESSING

Time to make: about 25 minutes

Serves 2

⅔ cup **bulgur wheat**

½ teaspoon **cumin seeds**

1 bunch **green onions**

⅓ cup **dried apricots**

¼ cup **dry-roasted cashews**

Dressing

2-inch piece **cucumber**

4 tablespoons **plain yogurt**

1 tablespoon **lemon juice**

Dash **ground red pepper**

1 tablespoon **olive oil**

1 tablespoon **chopped fresh mint**

Salt and freshly ground black pepper

Bulgur wheat is one of those ingredients that sits at the back of my kitchen cupboard until I suddenly notice it's nearly at its use-by date; then we eat bulgur with everything for a week. It's not that I don't like it; I just don't immediately consider it as an option when thinking up quick meals at the last minute. Testing for this book has reminded me of how simple it is to prepare and how good it is.

1   Heat a large, dry skillet over high heat until hot, then add the bulgur wheat and cumin seeds and stir until they are golden. Transfer to a bowl, pour 2½ cups boiling water over the bulgur and let stand for 20 minutes.

2   Chop the green onions and the apricots, then set aside.

3   Meanwhile, make the dressing. Grate the cucumber. Place the yogurt in a small bowl and stir until it is smooth. Add the cucumber, lemon juice, red pepper, olive oil, and mint. Season generously with salt and pepper. Mix until completely combined.

4   Rinse the soaked bulgur under cold water and drain well, squeezing out any excess moisture with your hands. Place in a serving bowl with the green onions, dried apricots, and cashews. Add the dressing; toss until well combined. Serve immediately.

Cook's Tip

This roasted bulgur wheat is also good served hot as an accompaniment. Add 1 tablespoon of olive oil and seasonings to the water used to soak the wheat. After the bulgur is hydrated, transfer it to an oven-safe dish and cover with aluminum foil. Bake at 400°F for 15 minutes until hot.

Nutrition facts per serving: 404 calories, 16 g total fat (3 g saturated fat), 2 mg cholesterol, 103 mg sodium, 60 g carbohydrate, 14 g fiber, 12 g protein.
Daily Values: 25% vitamin A, 25% vitamin C, 9% calcium, 32% iron.

QUICK EGG-FRIED RICE

Time to make: 5 minutes
Time to cook: about 20 minutes

Serves 3

6 green onions

1 cup brown or button mushrooms

½ green bell pepper

1 cup uncooked jasmine rice, about 3 cups cooked if you use leftover rice

1 teaspoon sesame oil

2 eggs

2 tablespoons sunflower oil

1 cup bean sprouts

⅓ cup frozen peas, thawed

2 tablespoons soy sauce

I think this dish is best made with rice cooked the day before, as it is drier and the final result is less sticky than if you use freshly cooked rice. I always cook extra rice and store it in the refrigerator so that I can make fried rice for my children, as it's a real favorite with them. This is my Chinese version—if we've had a rice pilaf with curry the night before, I just add extra vegetables and stir in 1 to 2 tablespoons mango chutney and some shredded coconut before heating it through to make an Indian version.

1 To prepare the vegetables, chop the green onions and slice the mushrooms. Core, seed, and chop the green pepper half.
2 Bring a large saucepan of water to a boil over high heat. Add the rice, lower the heat and simmer 10 minutes until tender. Drain, rinse under cold water to cool and drain again. Pat dry with paper towels.
3 Meanwhile, place the sesame oil in a small bowl and whisk in the eggs; set aside.
4 Heat the oil in a wok or deep skillet over high heat until almost smoking. Add the green onions, mushrooms, and green pepper; stir-fry 3 minutes. Add bean sprouts and peas. Continue stir-frying 1 minute more or until the vegetables are crisp-tender.
5 Stir in the rice and stir-fry 3 to 5 minutes until thoroughly heated through. Add the beaten eggs and stir gently until set, then stir in the soy sauce until completely mixed. Serve immediately.

Nutrition facts per serving: 408 calories, 14 g total fat (2 g saturated fat), 142 mg cholesterol, 746 mg sodium, 57 g carbohydrate, 2 g fiber, 12 g protein.
Daily Values: 13% vitamin A, 34% vitamin C, 4% calcium, 30% iron.

VEGETABLE BIRYANI

Time to make: about 5 minutes
Time to cook: about 25 minutes

Serves 4

1 small onion

1 small carrot

1 small parsnip

¼ small cauliflower

1 tablespoon sunflower oil

**½ cup green beans, cut in
half crosswise**

1 to 2 tablespoons biryani paste

¾ cup basmati rice

**½ cup canned chopped
tomatoes (undrained)**

1½ cups vegetable stock or broth

**Salt and freshly ground
black pepper**

**Toasted flaked almonds,
raisins, and fresh cilantro,
to garnish**

This rice dish is an excellent choice if you suddenly have to cook for a large number of people at the last minute, as you can use any selection of seasonal vegetables that you have in the kitchen. To save time, I use an excellent ready-made biryani paste that I buy at the supermarket, which makes a delicious spicy dish that isn't too fiery. As long as I always have some, along with a ready supply of basmati rice, I feel confident that I have the basis for a satisfying meal at any time. I serve this with a yogurt raita and a selection of chutneys.

1   To prepare the vegetables, finely chop the onion, peel and cut the carrot and parsnip into chunks, and break the cauliflower into flowerets.
2   Heat the oil in a large saucepan over medium heat. Add the onion, carrot, and parsnip and cook 5 minutes, stirring occasionally, until lightly browned. Stir in the cauliflower and green beans and continue cooking 1 minute more.
3   Stir in the biryani paste and rice and cook 1 minute. Add the undrained tomatoes, stock or broth, salt, and pepper. Bring to a boil, cover and cook 15 to 18 minutes until the liquid is absorbed and the rice is tender.
4   To serve, fluff the rice with a fork and garnish with almonds, raisins, and fresh cilantro.

Cook's Tip
Soaking the basmati rice before cooking it produces a lighter, less sticky grain, but it does make the recipe longer than 30 minutes to prepare. If you have the time, however, rinse the rice until the water runs clear, then soak it in 2½ cups of water for about 30 minutes. Drain and use as directed in the recipe.

Nutrition facts per serving: 217 calories, 6 g total fat (1 g saturated fat), 0 mg cholesterol, 568 mg sodium, 39 g carbohydrate, 3 g fiber, 4 g protein.
Daily Values: 35% vitamin A, 38% vitamin C, 4% calcium, 18% iron.

Vegetable Biryani

SWEET AND SOUR ROOT VEGETABLES WITH COUSCOUS

Time to make: 5 minutes
Time to cook: 25 minutes

Serves 3

1 cup couscous

2 tablespoons olive oil

1 red onion, sliced

1 garlic clove, minced

1 parsnip, peeled and sliced

1 carrot, peeled and sliced

4 ounces rutabaga, peeled and cubed

¼ teaspoon ground cinnamon

¼ teaspoon ground ginger

½ teaspoon paprika

1¼ cups vegetable stock

Salt and freshly ground black pepper

1 tablespoon honey

1 tablespoon balsamic or red wine vinegar

1½ tablespoons chopped fresh rosemary

Couscous is often mistakenly referred to as a grain but is, in fact, a pasta made from flour and rolled into characteristic tiny balls. Most of the couscous you buy only needs soaking to swell the grains, then it can be steamed or warmed through in a covered pan. I prefer the steamed method. A steamer pan that includes a steamer basket or colander that fits over the top works best with this dish. Or, use a large pot that is large enough to accommodate a colander when covered.

1 Place the couscous in a bowl and sprinkle with ¾ cup cold water. Let stand 15 minutes, stirring occasionally to break up any lumps.
2 While couscous is soaking, heat half of the oil in a large pot over low heat. Add the onion and garlic; cook 3 minutes, stirring occasionally, until the onion is softened but not brown. Stir in the parsnip, carrot, rutabaga, cinnamon, ginger, and paprika; cook over high heat until the vegetables are just golden, 2 to 3 minutes.
3 Stir in the stock, salt, and pepper. Bring to a boil, then reduce the heat. Cover and simmer about 10 minutes.
4 Place the couscous in a colander. Set colander over the vegetable mixture. Cover and allow couscous to steam atop the vegetables for 5 minutes.
5 Remove the colander of couscous; set aside. Stir the honey, vinegar, and rosemary into the vegetable mixture. Replace the colander of couscous over the vegetables. Return the vegetable mixture to a boil. Cook about 5 minutes or until the liquid is reduced and syrupy.
6 Stir the remaining olive oil into the couscous. Place couscous into a shallow serving dish. Spoon the vegetables over the couscous and serve immediately.

Nutrition facts per serving: 427 calories, 10 g total fat (1 g saturated fat), 0 mg cholesterol, 485 mg sodium, 77 g carbohydrate, 15 g fiber, 10 g protein.
Daily Values: 485% vitamin A, 30% vitamin C, 6% calcium, 14% iron.

GREEN HERB RISOTTO

Time to make: 5 minutes
Time to cook: 25 minutes

Serves 3

3 cups vegetable stock or broth

1 shallot or small onion

1 garlic clove

1 tablespoon olive oil

1 cup arborio rice

4 tablespoons dry white wine

To finish

**3 tablespoons margarine
    or butter**

**1½ cups fresh mixed herbs,
    such as flat-leaf parsley,
    basil, chives, tarragon, dill,
    or chervil**

**3 tablespoons freshly grated
    Parmesan cheese**

**Salt and freshly ground
    black pepper**

Risottos are my idea of the perfect comfort food. Rich, creamy, and intensely satisfying both to cook and eat, they brighten up the darkest winter evening for me. I make risottos in all the colors of the rainbow, just by following the basic method and adding a vegetable flavoring. Pumpkin, eggplant, and zucchini are all favorite ingredients. This aromatic version was inspired by my friend Paul Gayler, chef at the Lanesborough Hotel in London, who has done so much to bring vegetarian food into the '90s.

1 Heat the stock or broth. Keep warm while preparing the vegetables.
2 Finely chop the shallot or onion. Mince the garlic. Heat the oil in a heavy-based saucepan. Add the shallot or onion and garlic and cook about 3 minutes until softened. Add the rice and stir until each grain is coated in oil.
3 Add a ladleful of hot stock or broth and the wine and simmer over medium-low heat until the liquid is absorbed, stirring constantly. Continue adding the stock or broth, a few tablespoons at a time, stirring frequently, until all the liquid is absorbed and the rice is tender and creamy but still with a slight bite. This should take about 20 minutes.
4 While the rice is cooking, place the margarine or butter in a blender or food processor with the herbs; process until well blended together.
5 When the stock or broth is absorbed and the rice is tender, stir in the herb butter and Parmesan cheese. Add salt and pepper, if desired. Serve immediately.

Nutrition facts per serving: 447 calories, 21 g total fat (3 g saturated fat), 10 mg cholesterol, 1,277 mg sodium, 57 g carbohydrate, 1 g fiber, 11 g protein.
Daily Values: 30% vitamin A, 31% vitamin C, 13% calcium, 15% iron.

Egg and cheese dishes

Many new vegetarians make the mistake of replacing meat with too many dairy products, thus counteracting the benefits of what should be healthier eating. So make these cheese-based recipes for an occasional, rather than daily, treat.

ARTICHOKE, PIMIENTO, AND GREEN BEAN OMELET

Time to make: about 5 minutes
Time to cook: about 20 minutes

Serves 2

1 onion

½ cup green beans

1 large cooked potato

1 canned pimiento, drained

4 canned artichoke hearts, drained

3 tablespoons olive oil

3 eggs

Salt and freshly ground black pepper

This Spanish omelet (or tortilla, as it is called in Spain) is delicious with fresh eggs and makes a wonderful centerpiece for a picnic. I make it when I have leftover baked potatoes in the refrigerator. In fact, I frequently make extra so I can make this recipe the following day.

1 To prepare the vegetables, slice the onion, trim the green beans, peel and dice the cooked potato, and cut the pimiento into strips. Quarter the artichoke hearts.
2 Heat half of the oil in a skillet over medium heat. Add the onion and cook 3 minutes until softened.
3 Meanwhile, bring a saucepan of water to a boil over high heat and blanch the beans 2 minutes, then drain and rinse under cold water and drain again. Pat dry with paper towels and cut in half crosswise.
4 Add the potato and pimiento to the skillet and cook 3 minutes more, stirring occasionally. Add the artichokes and beans and continue cooking 3 minutes more, stirring occasionally.
5 Pour the vegetable mixture into a colander or sieve and drain for a few minutes to remove any excess oil.
6 Place the eggs, salt, and pepper in a bowl and beat well. Add the drained vegetables and mix together thoroughly.
7 Heat the remaining oil in an 8-inch skillet over medium heat. Add the egg mixture and cook until the eggs are set and the base is lightly browned, 4 to 5 minutes.
8 Place a plate over the pan and carefully turn out the omelet onto the plate, then slide it back into the pan and cook the other side for 3 minutes or until lightly browned. To serve, cut the omelet into wedges.

Nutrition facts per serving: 413 calories, 28 g total fat (5 g saturated fat), 320 mg cholesterol, 409 mg sodium, 29 g carbohydrate, 5 g fiber, 13 g protein.
Daily Values: 20% vitamin A, 42% vitamin C, 7% calcium, 17% iron.

Sliding Artichoke, Pimiento, and Green Bean Omelet onto a plate for serving

GREEN ONION AND GARBANZO BEAN OMELET

Time to make: about 3 minutes
Time to cook: 10 to 15 minutes

Serves 1

4 green onions

1 small garlic clove

½ tomato

1 tablespoon olive oil

½ cup canned garbanzo beans, drained and rinsed

3 eggs

Dash turmeric

1 tablespoon chopped fresh flat-leaf parsley

Salt and freshly ground black pepper

An omelet is one of those dishes that has to be just right for the person who's going to eat it—some like them runny in the center (me), others prefer a firm set. Ideally a good omelet should combine the two with a golden exterior concealing a moist, flavorful inside. An indifferent omelet, however, used to be the fate of many a vegetarian when eating out, but this is improving. I think it's well worth rediscovering the joys of a properly cooked version in your own home. Garbanzo beans add a welcome texture to this version. I particularly enjoy this with a simple tomato and onion salad.

1 To prepare the vegetables, chop the green onions and garlic. Seed and chop the tomato half.

2 Heat half the oil in a skillet over medium heat. Add the green onions, garlic, and garbanzo beans and cook 3 minutes, stirring occasionally, until the green onions are wilted. Remove from the pan and keep warm.

3 Place the eggs in a bowl with the turmeric, tomato, parsley, salt, and pepper. Beat together well.

4 Heat the remaining oil in the cleaned pan over medium heat. When it is hot, add the egg mixture and cook, stirring gently with a fork, until the base begins to set. Stop stirring and continue cooking until the base is golden.

5 Spoon the garbanzo bean mixture into the center, fold over the omelet and serve.

Nutrition facts per serving: 219 calories, 15 g total fat (3 g saturated fat), 320 mg cholesterol, 308 mg sodium, 9 g carbohydrate, 2 g fiber, 12 g protein.
Daily Values: 22% vitamin A, 27% vitamin C, 5% calcium, 16% iron.

FRIED POTATO PANCAKE WITH EGGS

Time to make: about 5 minutes
Time to cook: 20 to 25 minutes

Serves 2 to 3

1 pound waxy potatoes, such as round red or white potatoes

1 onion

2 garlic cloves

4 tablespoons olive oil

Salt and freshly ground black pepper

4 tablespoons chopped fresh flat-leaf parsley

2 to 3 eggs

When my husband and I are traveling through Southwest France, we really look forward to the wonderful local, crisp fried potato dish that makes a perfect accompaniment to fried eggs. There the cooks use goose fat, but I've found the dish works almost as well with olive oil. This is not a recipe for anyone watching fat levels, but as an occasional treat for brunch or supper, it's perfect. By using olive oil you will be reducing the saturated fat content in any case and, if you serve a green vegetable, such as green beans, and follow with fruit, your meal will be good for you and delicious.

1   To prepare the vegetables, thinly slice the potatoes and onion. Mince the garlic.
2   Heat the oil in a large deep skillet over medium to high heat until almost smoking. Add the potato and onion slices in batches, stirring to coat each batch in oil, and season well with salt and pepper. Cook, carefully lifting and turning the potatoes with a pancake turner, about 15 minutes until the potatoes are tender and just golden. Try not to let the potatoes break up too much— this will be a real problem if you use a potato with a starchy flesh.
3   Add the garlic and parsley to the pan and stir gently to combine. Flatten the potatoes into a pancake and continue cooking until the base is golden and crisp. Cut the pancake into 2 to 3 wedges and remove with a spatula; keep warm.
4   Fry the eggs in the oil remaining in the pan. To serve, arrange a cooked egg over the top of each wedge. Serve immediately.

Nutrition facts per serving: 368 calories, 22 g total fat (3 g saturated fat), 142 mg cholesterol, 102 mg sodium, 37 g carbohydrate, 2 g fiber, 8 g protein.
Daily Values: 9% vitamin A, 46% vitamin C, 4% calcium, 23% iron.

MUFFINS WITH GOAT CHEESE AND TARRAGON EGGS

Time to make: about 5 minutes
Time to cook: about 5 minutes

Serves 1 or 2

1 English muffin

2 teaspoons black olive paste (see Note, page 45) or dried tomato paste

2 eggs

1 tablespoon milk

1 tablespoon chopped fresh tarragon

Salt and freshly ground black pepper

1 tablespoon margarine or butter

1 ounce goat cheese

Fresh tarragon sprigs, to garnish

Mark and I spent the first night of our honeymoon in a beautiful country house hotel. One of the best things about the stay was the wonderful breakfast served outside under one of those huge canvas umbrellas that are now everywhere. At that time, I hadn't seen such a thing before and was instantly determined to have one. Be that as it may (we still don't have a fancy umbrella eight years later, though I do go to gardening shows and fantasize), the breakfast was delicious; scrambled eggs cooked with fresh tarragon, melt-in-the-mouth croissants and home-made apricot jam, and perfect coffee.

Tarragon is the ideal herb for eggs, so with that breakfast as inspiration, I came up with this. It makes a great snack or light supper for one, or a simple starter for a dinner for two.

1 Split the muffin in half and toast on both sides. Spread the cut sides with the olive or tomato paste.
2 Put the eggs in a small bowl and beat in the milk, tarragon, salt, and pepper.
3 Melt the margarine or butter in a small nonstick pan over medium heat. Add the egg mixture and cook, stirring occasionally, until the eggs begin to set but are still creamy.
4 Crumble in the cheese and stir it in until well mixed. Spoon the egg mixture over the muffin halves.
5 Serve immediately, garnished with a sprig of fresh tarragon.

Cook's Tip
For fish eaters, a little diced smoked salmon is wonderful added to the egg mixture.

Nutrition facts per serving: 482 calories, 29 g total fat (6 g saturated fat), 452 mg cholesterol, 947 mg sodium, 33 g carbohydrate, 2 g fiber, 22 g protein.
Daily Values: 38% vitamin A, 0% vitamin C, 18% calcium, 24% iron.

Muffins with Goat Cheese and Tarragon Eggs

CELERIAC AND STILTON SOUFFLÉS

Time to make: about 15 minutes
Time to cook: 12 to 15 minutes

Serves 2

8 ounces celeriac

2 tablespoons margarine
   or butter

¼ cup all-purpose flour

⅔ cup skim milk

1 cup Stilton cheese

4 eggs, separated

1 teaspoon Dijon-style mustard

Dash ground red pepper

Salt and freshly ground
   black pepper

1 tablespoon freshly grated
   Parmesan cheese

Celeriac is a root vegetable with a strong yet subtle flavor of celery. It makes a tasty partner to Stilton, here used together in a soufflé. Soufflés have a reputation for being difficult to make, but if you follow the steps carefully and don't open the oven door to check while it is cooking, you shouldn't go wrong.

1 Preheat the oven to 425°F. Grease two 4-inch soufflé dishes. Peel and finely dice the celeriac.

2 Bring a saucepan of water to a boil over high heat. Add the celeriac and cook 10 minutes until tender. Drain well, then puree in a food processor.

3 Meanwhile, melt the margarine or butter in a large saucepan over medium heat. Stir in the flour and cook, stirring constantly, 1 minute. Off the heat, gradually whisk in the milk, then return the pan to the heat. Bring to a boil, stirring constantly, to make a thick, smooth sauce.

4 Remove the pan from the heat, stir in the celeriac puree, and crumble in the Stilton, followed by the egg yolks, mustard, and seasonings. Beat together well.

5 Put the egg whites in a clean, dry bowl and whisk until stiff but not dry, then carefully fold them into the cheese and celeriac base.

6 Spoon the soufflé mixture evenly into the prepared dishes and sprinkle with Parmesan cheese. Bake 12 to 15 minutes until well risen and golden. Serve immediately.

Cook's Tip
This mixture will also make one large soufflé or fill six small ramekins; always remember to season any egg dish well to bring out the full flavor.

Nutrition facts per serving: 617 calories, 44 g total fat (24 g saturated fat), 516 mg cholesterol, 1,488 mg sodium, 22 g carbohydrate, 2 g fiber, 34 g protein.
Daily Values: 51% vitamin A, 11% vitamin C, 48% calcium, 18% iron.

BAKED EGGS WITH ASPARAGUS AND GREEN BEANS

Time to make: about 3 minutes
Time to cook: about 15 minutes

Serves 1

**1 tablespoon margarine
or butter**

**½ cup fresh asparagus tips, cut
diagonally into 1-inch pieces**

**½ cup green beans, cut
diagonally into 1-inch pieces**

2 tablespoons dry white wine

**Salt and freshly ground
black pepper**

1 large egg

**2 tablespoons crème fraîche
(see Note, page 87)**

**1 tablespoon chopped fresh
tarragon or chives**

**1 tablespoon freshly grated
Parmesan cheese**

If I really want to treat myself on one of the rare evenings I get to myself, this is the dish I prepare. It is so simple, yet the combination of flavors and textures is so satisfying I am hard pressed to come up with a better recipe. A glass of dry white wine, some good bread to mop up the juices, and a good book— what more could you ask for? Asparagus is available now most of the year around but, as you may have realized, I like cooking with seasonal produce. So ideally I would have to have my solitary evening during asparagus season.

1 Preheat the oven to 350°F.
2 Melt the margarine or butter in a small saucepan over medium heat until foaming. Add the vegetables and cook, stirring, for 1 minute, then add the wine and simmer 2 minutes more until the asparagus and beans are almost tender. Add salt and pepper.
3 Arrange the vegetable mixture over the base of an individual casserole dish. Break the egg over the top of the vegetables and spoon the crème fraîche evenly over the egg and vegetables. Sprinkle with tarragon or chives, Parmesan cheese, and, if desired, salt and pepper.
4 Bake until the egg is just set, about 12 minutes. Serve immediately.

Cook's Tip
Sugar snap peas or fresh shelled peas work well with the asparagus in this recipe.

Nutrition facts per serving: 348 calories, 27 g total fat (9 g saturated fat), 245 mg cholesterol, 431 mg sodium, 11 g carbohydrate, 3 g fiber, 13 g protein.
Daily Values: 45% vitamin A, 44% vitamin C, 14% calcium, 14% iron.

EGG AND CAULIFLOWER CURRY

Time to make: about 10 minutes
Time to cook: about 20 minutes

Serves 2

4 eggs

1 tablespoon sunflower oil

½ small onion, chopped

1 garlic clove, minced

½ teaspoon grated fresh
gingerroot

1 tablespoon medium curry paste

1 teaspoon tomato paste

1 tablespoon lemon juice

Salt

⅔ cup vegetable stock or broth

2 cups cauliflower flowerets

4 tablespoons plain yogurt

3 tablespoons chopped
fresh cilantro

I must admit that cauliflower as a vegetable served on its own is not a favorite of mine, as I find it somewhat dull. Add a creamy, well-flavored sauce, however, and the vegetable is transformed. Cauliflower curry is a great speedy supper, and in this recipe the distinctive texture and subtle flavor of cauliflower are enhanced by a lightly spiced sauce.

A year or two ago I would have rejected the idea of using a purchased curry paste, but with the huge improvement in quality of those available, I now keep a jar handy for when I'm in a hurry or away from my own kitchen—I tested this recipe while on a family vacation when I certainly didn't want to buy lots of new spices. All this needs in the way of accompaniments are plain boiled rice and a green vegetable.

1 Place the eggs in a small saucepan, cover with cold water and bring to a boil over high heat. Reduce heat; simmer, covered, 8 minutes. Run the eggs under cold water until they are cool. Shell the eggs and cut them in half, then set aside while you prepare the sauce.

2 Heat the oil in a saucepan over medium heat. Add the onion and cook 5 minutes, stirring occasionally, until golden. Stir in the garlic, ginger, and curry paste and stir-fry 1 minute, then stir in the tomato paste, lemon juice, salt, and vegetable stock or broth.

3 Bring the mixture to a boil, then add the cauliflower flowerets, reduce the heat, cover and simmer 8 to 10 minutes until the cauliflower is just tender.

4 Stir about half the hot mixture into the yogurt. Return mixture to saucepan. Add the cilantro. Add the eggs to the sauce, cut sides down, and heat through gently, taking care not to let the sauce boil.

Nutrition facts per serving: 288 calories, 19 g total fat (4 g saturated fat), 428 mg cholesterol, 787 mg sodium, 16 g carbohydrate, 4 g fiber, 17 g protein.
Daily Values: 27% vitamin A, 94% vitamin C, 15% calcium, 31% iron.

Egg and Cauliflower Curry

CAMEMBERT AND CRANBERRY PARCELS

Time to make: 5 minutes
Time to cook: 15 to 20 minutes

Serves 4

**6 ounces Camembert or
Brie cheese**

**2 tablespoons margarine
or butter**

**2 sheets phyllo pastry, each
about 17 x 12 inches, cut in
half crosswise**

2 tablespoons cranberry sauce

There was a time when French soft cheese seemed to appear everywhere, either *en croûte* or deep fried, usually accompanied by a dollop of gooseberry jam. I thought the fad had all but disappeared, but then I spotted a rendition on a wine bar menu recently and remembered how delicious the combination of melted, gooey cheese and crisp coating could be. I make this with ready-made phyllo pastry but puff pastry works just as well. Serve with a salad of bitter leaves, such as radicchio or frisée, and a sharp dressing.

1   Preheat the oven to 425°F. Cut the cheese into 4 wedges.
2   Melt the margarine or butter. Brush each sheet of phyllo pastry with melted margarine or butter, then fold it in half. Place a piece of cheese in the center of each sheet of phyllo pastry and top with a dollop of cranberry sauce. Either wrap the pastry around the cheese to form a neat package, or bring the edges together at the top to form a bundle, twisting gently to seal.
3   Spray or sprinkle a baking sheet with cold water. Place the phyllo parcels on the pan and brush them with the remaining melted margarine or butter. Bake until the pastry is crisp and golden, or for 15 to 20 minutes. Serve immediately.

Nutrition facts per serving: 220 calories, 17 g total fat (8 g saturated fat), 30 mg cholesterol, 474 mg sodium, 9 g carbohydrate, 0 g fiber, 9 g protein.
Daily Values: 19% vitamin A, 1% vitamin C, 14% calcium, 3% iron.

FRIED MOZZARELLA AND PESTO SANDWICHES

Time to make: 10 minutes
Time to cook: 8 minutes

Serves 2

5 ounces mozzarella cheese, preferably buffalo

4 thick slices Italian or French bread

2 teaspoons purchased pesto sauce

Salt and freshly ground black pepper

1 egg

2 to 3 tablespoons olive oil

With the ever-increasing availability of interesting specialty breads, sandwiches have taken a big step forward. I enjoy the variety of so many of the once-rare, but now widely-available, ingredients. Fried mozzarella sandwiches are a favorite with my family for Sunday night. Served with a big green salad and a glass of red wine for a light supper, they make a satisfying end to the weekend.

1 Cut the mozzarella into thin slices. Remove the crusts from the bread slices.

2 Spread the pesto sauce on 2 slices of bread, then top with the mozzarella cheese slices and season to taste. Top with another slice of bread and press firmly together.

3 Crack the egg into a shallow dish. Add salt. With a fork beat the egg slightly. Carefully dip the sandwiches into the beaten egg, turning to coat sandwiches on both sides.

4 Heat the oil in a large skillet. Add the sandwiches and cook over medium heat 3 to 4 minutes on each side; cook the sandwiches one at a time if your skillet isn't large enough. Drain the sandwiches on paper towels, cut into triangles and serve immediately.

Cook's Tip
Vary this recipe by using different types of breads and cheeses. Try Stilton cheese with walnut bread, Brie with olive bread or dried tomato bread, and even cheddar cheese with raisin bread. Look for these and other types of breads at specialty bakeries.

Nutrition facts per serving: 565 calories, 37 g total fat (12 g saturated fat), 162 mg cholesterol, 775 mg sodium, 35 g carbohydrate, 0 g fiber, 23 g protein.
Daily Values: 21% vitamin A, 1% vitamin C, 37% calcium, 16% iron.

Desserts

Some people express surprise that a book on vegetarian cookery would include sweet recipes. Still, I don't see why vegetarians should have to buy a separate book for desserts. Admittedly, I rarely make a dessert midweek unless we have a guest—we usually have fruit with thick yogurt—but these are the recipes I use when I feel like having a special treat.

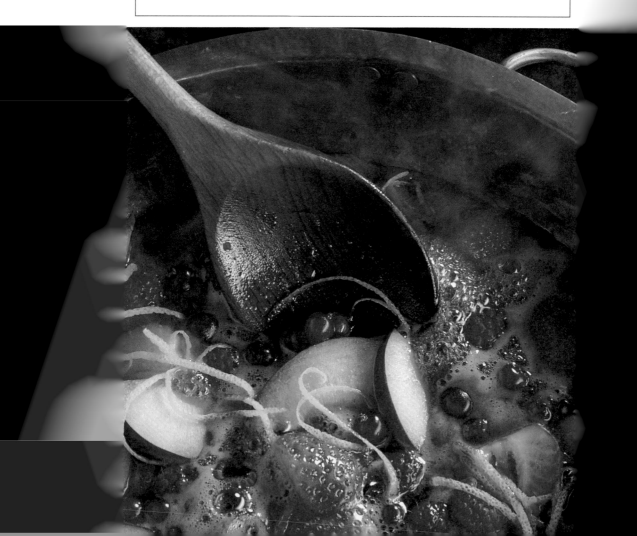

RED FRUIT FLAMBÉ

Time to make: about 5 minutes
Time to cook: 10 to 15 minutes

Serves 2

1 cup fresh strawberries

2 ounces plums

1 ounce red currants

1 orange

1 cup fresh raspberries

2 tablespoons brandy or rum

Vanilla ice cream or crème fraîche *

When at its best, fresh, soft summer fruit needs little enhancement. But, if I have some that is a little past its peak, this quick dessert makes good use of it. If you are worried about setting fire to the kitchen or singeing your eyebrows, omit the flambéing and simmer the fruit for one minute after adding the brandy.

1 To prepare the fruits, halve the strawberries; halve and pit the plums, then thinly slice them; and remove the currants from their strings. Finely grate the orange rind and squeeze the juice.
2 Put the strawberries, plums, red currants, orange rind, and raspberries in a bowl and mix together.
3 Put the sugar in a heavy-based shallow pan or skillet over high heat and heat until it melts and starts to caramelize and turn brown. Don't stir it as it melts or it will form sticky lumps—just move the pan around on the burner to distribute the heat. This will take about 3 minutes.
4 Stir in the orange juice—watch out for spattering sugar—then lower the heat and continue stirring until the mixture is syrupy.
5 Add the fruit to the pan and stir over medium heat until heated through, 3 to 4 minutes. Add the brandy to the pan and light with a long match. Shake the pan until the flames die down, then serve at once with vanilla ice cream or crème fraîche.

* Note:
Make crème fraîche by heating 1 cup *whipping cream* in a saucepan over low heat until warm (90° to 100°). Pour warm cream into a small bowl. Stir in 2 tablespoons *buttermilk*. Cover; let stand at room temperature for 24 to 30 hours or until thickened. *Do not stir.* Store in a covered container in the refrigerator for up to 1 week. Stir before serving. Makes 1 cup.

Nutrition facts per serving: 360 calories, 8 g total fat (5 g saturated fat), 29 mg cholesterol, 55 mg sodium, 63 g carbohydrate, 6 g fiber, 4 g protein.
Daily Values: 10% vitamin A, 149% vitamin C, 10% calcium, 6% iron.

Bubbling Red Fruit Flambé ready for serving

APRICOT AND LEMON PUDDINGS

Time to make: about 8 minutes
Time to bake: 12 to 15 minutes

Serves 2

¾ cup self-rising flour, plus
    extra for flouring the
    work surface

2 tablespoons margarine or
    butter, well chilled, plus
    extra for greasing the
    ramekins

1 tablespoon superfine sugar

¼ cup rice flour

1 teaspoon grated lemon rind

2 to 3 tablespoons skim milk,
    plus a little extra for glazing

1 tablespoon sliced almonds

Heavy cream, optional

Filling

1 7-ounce can apricots
    (packed in own juice)

1 tablespoon brown sugar

When I was a child, my family and I used to visit a favorite restaurant in a Tudor farmhouse. It served the most wonderful traditional English food, the type now served in trendy restaurants across the country. I remember that the desserts were particularly good, especially the apricot pie. It was intensely fruity with a crust that was more like a biscuit than pastry. This is my quick homage to that pie.

1 Preheat the oven to 400°F. Grease 2 large ramekins.
2 Sift the flour into a mixing bowl. Dice the margarine or butter, then rub it into the flour with your fingertips until the mixture resembles fine bread crumbs.
3 Stir in the sugar, rice flour, and lemon rind, then add enough milk to make a soft dough.
4 Turn out the dough onto a lightly floured work surface and roll out until it is about ¾-inch thick. Use a fluted cookie cutter to cut out two 3½-inch rounds.
5 Divide the apricots and their juice between the ramekins. Sprinkle with sugar.
6 Top each pudding with a dough round and brush with a little milk, then sprinkle almonds over the top.
7 Bake the puddings until the topping is well risen and golden, 12 to 15 minutes. Serve with heavy cream, if you like.

Cook's Tip
You can use any canned fruit for this dessert, but be sure not to use any fruit packed in a syrup, as the end result will be too sweet.

Nutrition facts per serving: 471 calories, 14 g total fat (3 g saturated fat), 1 mg cholesterol, 744 mg sodium, 78 g carbohydrate, 8 g fiber, 8 g protein.
Daily Values: 36% vitamin A, 12% vitamin C, 18% calcium, 19% iron.

HOT MOCHA SOUFFLÉS

Time to make: about 10 minutes
Time to cook: 12 to 15 minutes

Serves 2

1 tablespoon superfine sugar

1 ounce semisweet chocolate

**2 tablespoons crème fraîche
(see Note, page 87)**

**¼ teaspoon instant coffee
granules**

2 eggs, separated

½ tablespoon brandy or rum

**Confectioners' sugar,
for dusting**

A hot chocolate soufflé is my emergency standby if we have unexpected guests—it's quick and simple. I usually have all of the ingredients, and everybody loves it. It's based on chocolate melted with cream, which gives an intense flavor. I like really bitter chocolate, so I suggest you use a dark chocolate with a high percentage of cocoa solids and throw in a little coffee and brandy for added kick. Prepare the base before the meal, then whisk up the egg whites and fold them in as soon as you finish eating. The soufflés take about 15 minutes to cook.

1 Preheat the oven to 400°F. Grease 2 ramekins and dust with half the superfine sugar. Finely chop the chocolate.
2 Place the chocolate, crème fraîche, and coffee together in a small saucepan over low heat and heat gently, stirring, until the chocolate melts. Remove the pan from the heat.
3 Stir the egg yolks and brandy or rum into the chocolate mixture until well mixed.
4 Put the egg whites in a bowl and beat until stiff but not dry, then beat in the remaining sugar. Lightly fold the egg whites into the chocolate mixture.
5 Divide the soufflé mixture between the prepared ramekins and place them in a roasting pan half-filled with hot water. Bake until puffed up, 12 to 15 minutes. Dust with confectioners' sugar and serve immediately.

Cook's Tip
To get the lightest results, make sure the eggs are at room temperature and the bowl is completely clean before beating the egg whites.

Nutrition facts per serving: 221 calories, 14 g total fat (7 g saturated fat), 226 mg cholesterol, 70 mg sodium, 17 g carbohydrate, 1 g fiber, 8 g protein.
Daily Values: 14% vitamin A, 0% vitamin C, 3% calcium, 8% iron.

BLACK CURRANT AND RASPBERRY SHERBET

Time to make: about 20 minutes,
plus up to 1 hour freezing

Serves 2

1 cup frozen black currants

Scant 1 cup frozen raspberries

3 tablespoons superfine sugar

1 tablespoon kirsch (optional)

1 egg white*

Mint sprigs, to garnish

Amaretti cookies or ladyfingers

This method of making an instant sherbet was shown to me by Prue Leith when I was a student at her cookery school in London. I have been making variations on the theme ever since, and as a recipe, its adaptability and ease of preparation made it an obvious choice for this book.

Make this just before you sit down to eat and return it to the freezer while eating your main course; it will be soft and scoopable when you need to serve it.

1 Remove the currants and raspberries from the freezer and let sit at room temperature to soften slightly, 15 minutes.
2 Put the black currants and raspberries in a blender or food processor. Add the sugar and kirsch, if using, and process until smooth but still icy.
3 Place the egg white in a bowl and beat until stiff. Fold beaten egg white into the fruit puree with a large metal spoon.
4 Transfer the mixture to a rigid container and freeze for up to 1 hour or until firm. To serve, scoop sherbet into dessert dishes and garnish with mint sprigs. Accompany with amaretti cookies or ladyfingers.

Cook's Tip
Eat this sherbet within a day or two, as the quality will deteriorate quickly because the fruit has been frozen twice. For a firmer set, make the sherbet without the alcohol, which inhibits freezing.

*Note
Young children, older adults, or those who are ill or have an immune system deficiency should avoid eating raw eggs.

Nutrition facts per serving: 147 calories, 1 g total fat (0 g saturated fat), 0 mg cholesterol, 29 mg sodium, 35 g carbohydrate, 5 g fiber, 3 g protein.
Daily Values: 2% vitamin A, 194% vitamin C, 3% calcium, 8% iron.

Black Currant and Raspberry Sherbet

FRESH RASPBERRY CRISP

Time to make: 10 minutes, plus
  cooling
Time to cook: 20 minutes

Serves 2

⅔ cup rolled oats

2 tablespoons brown sugar

1 tablespoon slivered almonds

1 teaspoon sesame seeds

1 to 2 tablespoons honey

⅓ cup plain yogurt

**2 tablespoons mascarpone
  cheese***

1 cup fresh raspberries

Raspberries and mint leaves

*Note
Mascarpone is an Italian
double- or triple-cream
cheese made from cow's
milk. Look for it in the
cheese section of your
supermarket or check an
Italian market.

I make up a quantity of this oat mixture and serve it with yogurt and fruit for breakfast or sprinkled over fresh fruit and baked like a crumble. It is a bit of a push to get the oat mixture roasted and cooled within the 30-minute limit, but it's so simple that I've included it anyway, as the oats can continue cooling while you enjoy your main course, and the dessert can be assembled at the last minute. If you do make up the oat mixture in advance, it will keep for up to one month in an airtight container.

1 Preheat the oven to 325°F. Put the oats, sugar, almonds, sesame seeds, and honey in a bowl and mix together.
2 Place the mixture in a small roasting pan and bake 20 minutes, stirring occasionally, until the mixture is crisp and golden. Spread out on a plate or tray and let cool.
3 Just before serving, stir the yogurt and mascarpone cheese together. Place a few raspberries in 2 tall glasses, sprinkle with some of the oat mixture and top with some of the yogurt mixture.
4 Continue layering, finishing with the yogurt mixture. Decorate with additional raspberries and mint and serve.

Cook's Tip
If raspberries aren't available, I sometimes use peaches and gingersnap cookies in the same way. Layer a couple of peeled and diced ripe peaches, crushed gingersnap cookies (about 4), and crème fraîche.

Nutrition facts per serving: 340 calories, 12 g total fat (5 g saturated fat), 20 mg cholesterol, 65 mg sodium, 53 g carbohydrate, 6 g fiber, 11 g protein.
Daily Values: 2% vitamin A, 26% vitamin C, 9% calcium, 13% iron.

BAKED AMARETTI PEACHES

Time to make: about 5 minutes
Time to cook: 15 to 20 minutes

Serves 2

2 large ripe peaches

4 amaretti cookies or large macaroons

1 egg yolk

2 tablespoons brandy, orange liqueur, or orange juice

Ice cream or plain yogurt (optional)

Amaretti cookies are those little almond cookies in multi-colored papers which, it seemed, were always served at the end of meals in Italian restaurants when I was a child. My sisters and I always looked for them, not because of the cookies inside but for the papers themselves. They were transformed by some magic of my mother's into little cones which she then set alight, and we would watch open-mouthed as they floated up to the ceiling, burning brightly. The friendly Italian proprietor must have viewed our arrival in his premises with trepidation as he ran to check his fire insurance! Anyway, the cookies make a quick flavoring for baked peaches; serve with best quality vanilla ice cream for a real treat.

1 Preheat the oven to 350°F. Halve the peaches, twist to separate the halves and carefully remove the pits. Lightly crush the cookies.
2 Place the halved peaches on a baking sheet.
3 Put the crushed cookies in a bowl with the egg yolk and mix together.
4 Spoon the mixture into the cavity in the peach halves left by the pits. Sprinkle with the liqueur or orange juice.
5 Bake until the peaches are just tender, 15 to 20 minutes. Serve warm with ice cream or yogurt.

Cook's Tip
Amaretti cookies are available in Italian supermarkets or look in the Italian section of your supermarket.

Nutrition facts per serving: 335 calories, 12 g total fat (1 g saturated fat), 107 mg cholesterol, 16 mg sodium, 49 g carbohydrate, 4 g fiber, 5 g protein.
Daily Values: 27% vitamin A, 23% vitamin C, 2% calcium, 5% iron.

PEAR BATTER PUDDING

Time to make: 10 minutes
Time to cook: 15 to 20 minutes

Serves 2

2 small, ripe pears

1 large egg

⅓ cup light cream

1 tablespoon superfine sugar

1 tablespoon ground almonds

1 tablespoon rum

Dash ground cinnamon

**1 tablespoon margarine
    or butter**

Confectioners' sugar, to dust

I've been experimenting recently with different ways to use basic pancake batter, and this is one of the results. It is like a French clafouti, but the end result is far richer, and I think it makes a splendid end to any meal. Cook this in a simple, shallow gratin dish, dust with confectioners' sugar and you have a dessert fit for a king.

1 Preheat the oven to 400°F. Peel, core, and slice the pears.
2 Arrange the pears into 2 shallow, individual casseroles.
3 Place the egg, cream, sugar, ground almonds, rum, and cinnamon in a bowl and beat together. Melt the margarine or butter and stir it into the batter.
4 Pour the batter over the pear slices. Bake until puffy, 15 to 18 minutes or till set. Sift confectioners' sugar over the top and serve immediately.

Nutrition facts per serving: 277 calories, 15 g total fat (5 g saturated fat), 121 mg cholesterol, 114 mg sodium, 29 g carbohydrate, 4 g fiber, 6 g protein.
Daily Values: 17% vitamin A, 8% vitamin C, 7% calcium, 6% iron.

INDEX

Metric Cooking Hints

By making a few conversions, cooks in Australia, Canada, and the United Kingdom can use the recipes in *30-Minute Vegetarian Recipes* with confidence. The charts on this page provide a guide for converting measurements from the U.S. customary system, which is used throughout this book, to the imperial and metric systems. There also is a conversion table for oven temperatures to accommodate the differences in oven calibrations.

Volume and Weight: Americans traditionally use cup measures for liquid and solid ingredients. The chart (top right) shows the approximate imperial and metric equivalents. If you are accustomed to weighing solid ingredients, here are some helpful approximate equivalents.
■ 1 cup butter, castor sugar, or rice = 8 ounces = about 250 grams
■ 1 cup flour = 4 ounces = about 125 grams
■ 1 cup icing sugar = 5 ounces = about 150 grams
  Spoon measures are used for smaller amounts of ingredients. Although the size of the tablespoon varies slightly among countries, for practical purposes and for recipes in this book, a straight substitution is all that's necessary.
  Measurements made using cups or spoons should always be level, unless stated otherwise.

Product Differences: Most of the ingredients called for in the recipes in this book are available in English-speaking countries. However, some are known by different names. Here are some common American ingredients and their possible counterparts:
■ Sugar is granulated or caster sugar.
■ Powdered sugar is icing sugar.
■ All-purpose flour is plain household flour or white flour. When self-rising flour is used in place of all-purpose flour in a recipe that calls for leavening, omit the leavening agent (baking soda or baking powder) and salt.
■ Light corn syrup is golden syrup.
■ Cornstarch is cornflour.
■ Baking soda is bicarbonate of soda.
■ Vanilla is vanilla essence.
■ Green, red or yellow sweet peppers are capsicums.
■ Sultanas are golden raisins.

Useful Equivalents: U.S. = Aust./Br.

⅛ teaspoon = 0.5 ml
¼ teaspoon = 1 ml
½ teaspoon = 2 ml
1 teaspoon = 5 ml
1 tablespoon = 1 tablespoon
¼ cup = 2 tablespoons = 2 fluid ounces = 60 ml
⅓ cup = ¼ cup = 3 fluid ounces = 90 ml
½ cup = ⅓ cup = 4 fluid ounces = 120 ml

⅔ cup = ½ cup = 5 fluid ounces = 150 ml
¾ cup = ⅔ cup = 6 fluid ounces = 180 ml
1 cup = ¾ cup = 8 fluid ounces = 240 ml
1¼ cups = 1 cup
2 cups = 1 pint
1 quart = 1 litre
½ inch = 1.27 centimetres
1 inch = 2.54 centimetres

Baking Pan Sizes

American	Metric
8x1½-inch round baking pan	20x4-centimetre cake tin
9x1½-inch round baking pan	23x3.5-centimetre cake tin
11x7x1½-inch baking pan	28x18x4-centimetre baking tin
13x9x2-inch baking pan	30x20x3-centimetre baking tin
2-quart rectangular baking dish	30x20x3-centimetre baking tin
15x10x2-inch baking pan	30x25x2-centimetre baking tin (Swiss roll tin)
9-inch pie plate	22x4- or 23x4-centimetre pie plate
7- or 8-inch springform pan	18- or 20-centimetre springform or loose-bottom cake tin
9x5x3-inch loaf pan	23x13x7-centimetre or 2-pound narrow loaf tin or pâté tin
1½-quart casserole	1.5-litre casserole
2-quart casserole	2-litre casserole

Oven Temperature Equivalents

Fahrenheit Setting	Celsius Setting*	Gas Setting
300°F	150°C	Gas Mark 2 (slow)
325°F	160°C	Gas Mark 3 (moderately slow)
350°F	180°C	Gas Mark 4 (moderate)
375°F	190°C	Gas Mark 5 (moderately hot)
400°F	200°C	Gas Mark 6 (hot)
425°F	220°C	Gas Mark 7
450°F	230°C	Gas Mark 8 (very hot)
Broil		Grill

*Electric and gas ovens may be calibrated using Celsius. However, increase the Celsius setting 10 to 20 degrees when cooking above 160°C with an electric oven. For convection or forced-air ovens (gas or electric), lower the temperature setting 10°C when cooking at all heat levels.